The Synergy Church

The SYNERGY Church

A Strategy for Integrating Small Groups and Sunday School

MICHAEL C. MACK

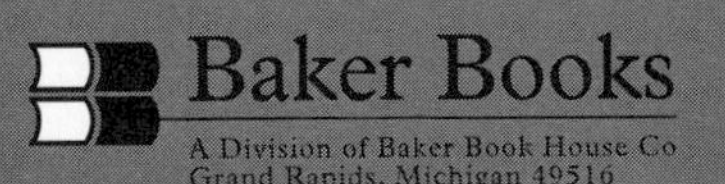
Baker Books
A Division of Baker Book House Co
Grand Rapids, Michigan 49516

Published by Baker Books
a division of Baker Book House Company
P.O. Box 6287, Grand Rapids, MI 49516-6287

Printed in the United States of America

Library of Congress Cataloging-in-Publication Data

Mack, Michael C., 1960–
The synergy church : a strategy for integrating small groups and Sunday school / Michael C. Mack.
p. cm.
Includes bibliographical references and index.
ISBN 0-8010-9009-1 (pbk.)
1. Church group work. 2. Small groups. 3. Sunday schools. I. Title.
BV652.2.M27 1996
268'.434—dc20 95-47637

Contents

FOREWORD

Churches have a tendency to view small groups as either a phenomenon or a program. But there is a growing awareness that small groups are more than what a church does: They are a mind set. The principles that undergird small groups must be the foundation upon which committees, ministries, work teams, and recovery groups are built. When small groups are viewed as a program, scarce resources of time and energy must be redirected from existing ministries in new directions. But when small groups are viewed as a mind set, existing ministries are transformed and maximized.

So it is timely that Michael Mack has written *The Synergy Church*. Churches that have struggled with the either-or questions involving small groups and Sunday school will be heartened to realize that the answer can be "both-and." Small groups and Sunday school can work hand in hand, fulfilling both similar and disparate functions within the body of Christ.

In this book, Michael relies on insightful research to offer both a practical guide and a thought-provoking text. I believe that this book will be useful to traditional churches implementing small group ministries, and to nontraditional churches examining how to effectively use their Sunday morning time in a wise and efficient manner. The result is that the mutual caring, prayer, encouragement, study, growth, and ministry that occur in group settings will infect both Sunday school and small group ministry.

I pray that God uses *The Synergy Church* to energize and revitalize existing ministries, and to encourage the creation of exciting, dynamic, relational ministries that will transform many lives for Jesus Christ, to the glory of God.

—Jeffrey Arnold

Introduction

"Small groups that meet in homes during the week for Bible study have become popular; some feel, at the expense of Sunday school enrollment," wrote Charles Arn, Donald McGavran, and Win Arn in 1987, documenting the opening of what some might consider a Pandora's box of questions about the future of the Sunday school. "Some members, subconsciously, are wondering whether the Sunday school is outdated. Others have quietly discussed how some churches are experimenting with restructuring the Sunday school hour."[1]

Today, as the popularity of small groups grows in larger and larger proportions, churches are faced with questions about what to do with their traditional adult Sunday school programs:

- Should small groups that meet in homes replace adult Sunday school?
- Which is more effective in evangelism and nurture?
- How can a small groups system be implemented in a traditional, Sunday school–based church?
- How can Sunday school and different types of small groups work together effectively?
- What will happen to the adult Sunday school in the church of the future?

- How can these ministries be integrated to achieve a synergistic, cooperative system for making and equipping disciples?

These are the main questions I will address in this book.

Form follows function. This is an important presupposition in this book. Before church forms, such as Sunday school and small groups, can be analyzed, church functions must be understood in the light of Scripture, culture, and history. Functions—evangelism and nurture and their components—are primary. Forms—Sunday school, small groups, and others—are not primary. When they become primary, they often also become "sacred."

Therefore, functions will be studied first, and then forms will be examined in light of those elementary functions. Church functions are to be examined in view of Scripture, of course, but they also must be examined in view of today's culture.

Church leaders should find this book helpful as they consider the essential functions of the church in today's society, and as they determine what mix of church forms can help their congregations be effective in making disciples and helping them grow in Christlikeness. Adult Sunday school and small groups are the main forms examined, although other structures will also be considered.

Gene Getz wrote *Sharpening the Focus of the Church* more than twenty years ago, but one of his statements summarizes well the purpose of this book:

> Once we develop a proper perspective Biblically, historically, and culturally, we must develop a contemporary strategy based particularly on New Testament principles; we must determine current needs in our own local church, formulate relevant objectives and goals, devise contemporary forms and structures, and use every legitimate resource to be a New Testament church in contemporary culture.[2]

This book will not try to define particular forms the church *must* use. The New Testament allows much freedom in the area of forms and structures. I will also not try to reinstitute specific forms found in the New Testament, but rather restore scriptural *functions* to the church and examine how some forms, particularly Sunday school and small groups, fit or do not fit those functions.

What would a restored biblical church look like? That is a primary question. The real questions are not whether Sunday school should be eliminated in favor of small groups, or if discipling groups should be instituted, or if traditional Sunday school classes should be replaced with electives, although all those questions will be considered. The main question is, How would a local congregation change current forms or institute new ones—if it needs to take such actions—in order to restore relational church functions as demonstrated in the New Testament and to relate to contemporary society?

The kind of restored church I am talking about is what Lyle Schaller refers to as the "seven-day-a-week church." In the introduction of his book by that title, he speaks about the emerging "full-service" church, or what I'll refer to later in this book as a "synergy" church:

> The big Protestant churches of the 1950s were built largely around the ecclesiastical trinity of that day—inspiring preaching, a superb choir, and an attractive Sunday school. For all practical purposes, these were Sunday morning churches. . . .
>
> The big Protestant church of today and tomorrow also is built around worship and memorable preaching, but . . . the Sunday school is but one component of a huge teaching ministry; and the schedule is filled with a variety of other events, classes, programs, and groups. These are the seven-day-a-week churches that are emerging as the successors to the big Sunday morning churches of the 1950s.[3]

Most churches today have a variety of groups—Sunday school, small fellowship groups, support and recovery groups, ministry groups. On their own, each of these groups may be effective. But in many cases these groups are not integrated in any way. There is often no system for helping people in their spiritual journeys to find the right groups to meet their needs and later to move into other groups as they grow. The typical church does not have enough leadership for all the good things it would like to do. There may be no systematic leadership training for the various groups.

The Synergy Church will help leaders organize and systematize the different groups in the church to help people begin the journey toward God, grow as disciples and responsible members of the body, and mature into leaders in the church.

Although this book focuses primarily on Sunday schools and small groups, these two ministries do not exist in a vacuum. Thus, the beginning chapters will be somewhat broad in perspective as the church is examined. The middle chapters will focus on Sunday school and small groups—analyzing them independently and then comparing them. The final chapters will again be broader, as a strategy for the church—with a variety of ministry options—is suggested. The research will be presented showing the wide-angle scene first to give perspective, and then zooming in on the main subjects—Sunday school and small groups—to show their particular relationships to the whole, and finally panning back out to a wide-angle view in order to show how the picture looks in the end.

It is assumed that the reader has a fairly good understanding of the philosophy and methodology for Sunday school and small group ministry. This is not a how-to-organize-and-run-an-efficient-small-group book. Many resources are available about how to start a small group, the components of a small group meeting, how to be a small group leader, and so forth. Many of these resources are given in the bibliography.

Forms of leadership—that is, the model for and the makeup and roles of the ministerial staff, elders, committees, and so forth—will not be discussed in great detail. This topic, especially as it relates to small group ministry, is handled in other works. One such book is *Prepare Your Church for the Future,* by Carl George. At the same time, it is not assumed that the functions of the church work independently of leadership. Roles of staff ministers, elders, and nonstaff leadership will be discussed as they relate to particular areas of the research, but a leadership model, such as George and others suggest, will not be given.

This book is by no means a panacea for all the ills of the church. There is no right way of doing Sunday school and small groups. Every church will find its own model depending on its own set of circumstances. The church is comprised of people, not programs. The day-to-day interworkings of the body require sensitivity to people's needs, especially as forms of the church are changing. While this book cannot give a solution or a model for each church's life, it can lay down some principles and strategies to be considered in carrying out the Lord's mission for his church.

PART 1

The BIG PICTURE

1

What's the Purpose?

Where there is no vision, the people perish.

Solomon
Proverbs 29:18 KJV

Suppose one of you wants to build a tower. Will he not first sit down and estimate the cost?

Jesus
Luke 14:28

Run in such a way as to get the prize. . . . I do not run like a man running aimlessly.

Paul
1 Corinthians 9:24–26

If you don't know where you're going, you might end up someplace else.

Pogo
Pogo comic strip

Each of these famous "philosophers" was talking about purpose or mission, and each message is the same: Without a clearly defined purpose or mission statement, whatever you're doing is destined to fail. That's true in the business world. It's true in sports. It's true for armies. And it is true for the church.

Businesses that are successful are constantly asking two key questions: What are we supposed to be doing? How well are we doing it?

Churches that regularly ask the same questions will be successful as well—successful, that is, in being the incarnation of God in the world, carrying out Christ's commission for his church to the glory of the Father. A church that does not understand its mission eventually becomes a cold, stiff organization run by people and programs, rather than an organism empowered by the Spirit of God to do his work in the world.

Where Are We Going?

Bible study groups, men's ministries, women's ministries, singles' ministries, recovery groups, Sunday school classes, prayer groups, seniors' ministries—every church, even the smallest, has a variety of programs going on. By design each of these groups focuses on a different thing. So what's to keep these groups—and the church as a whole—from going in dozens of different directions? *Purpose.* The church that has a clearly defined mission statement knows where it is going. All of the groups and programs of the church can then be evaluated according to that mission statement. In an effective congregation every program channels together and is directed toward the goal.

Programs in ineffective congregations function independently of the church's mission. Each carries out its own ministry with little understanding as to how that service fits into the overall mission of the church. Many opportunities can be taken advantage of when each group has a vision for the big picture.

So what is God's mission for his church? The question here is, *Why* does the church exist? The mission will then determine the strategy (functions) a church will undertake.

The next question is, *How* will the church accomplish this purpose? The strategies then determine the structure of the church, which includes church forms. That leads to the next question: *What* organizational forms suit the strategy?

Often the church has reversed this process. It begins with the existing or fashionable structures and then tries to design its mission around those structures.

Form follows function. This maxim is foundational for any endeavor. "Yet in the church, practices, programs, procedures, and building styles are handed down as traditional forms," says Joe Ellis. "It is frequently a challenge to find ways to function within these forms to achieve some measure of success in fulfilling the real purpose of the church."[1]

What Is Our Primary Mission?

Before we can really understand the primary mission of the church we need to understand God's purpose for his world. Charles Arn, Donald McGavran, and Win Arn put it this way:

> Scripture bears this clear testimony: God's unswerving purpose is that lost mankind be redeemed and brought into His church. Christ's birth, crucifixion, and resurrection were for the purpose that mankind might be saved.
>
> Christ opened a way of salvation so that all people, everywhere, might find forgiveness of sin, reconciliation to God, new life in Christ, and become members of His Body—the Church. This primary purpose of God, proclaimed by Christ's disciples, is the motivation and power behind growing churches.
>
> That God purposes the redemption of lost mankind is the testimony of Scripture in its entirety.[2]

With the incarnation, Jesus took on a human body. His mission was "not to do my will but to do the will of him who sent me. . . . For my Father's will is that everyone who looks to the Son and believes in him shall have eternal life" (John 6:38, 40). Jesus told Pilate, "For this reason I was born, and for this I came into the world, to testify to the truth" (John 18:37). The truth he testified to is summed up in John 14:6: "I am the way and the truth and the life. No one comes to the Father except through me."

Jesus' mission was to reconcile humankind with the Father. Paul writes in 1 Timothy, "God is on one side and all the people on the other side, and Christ Jesus, Himself man, is between them to bring them together, by giving His life for all mankind. This is the message which at the proper time God gave to the world" (2:5–6 TLB).

Just as in the incarnation Jesus came into the world, with his ascension he has taken on a new body, the church. Paul refers to the church as Christ's body numerous times in his letters. In Ephesians 1:22–23 Paul says, "God placed all things under [Christ's] feet and appointed him to be head over everything for the church, which is his body." The church is then Jesus' continued incarnation of the Father on earth. That is what the apostle Paul means when he says "we are therefore Christ's ambassadors, as though God were making his appeal through us" (2 Cor. 5:20).

Jesus prepared his followers to continue his earthly mission before he returned to heaven. "As the Father has sent me, I am sending you," he told them (John 20:21). The specifics of the mission are found in Matthew 28:18–20—as well as Mark 16:15–16; Luke 24:46–49; John 20:21–23; and Acts 1:8. At the heart of the Great Commission is the making of disciples.

In the Book of Ephesians the apostle Paul helps us discern God's purpose for his church. He spells it out for the Ephesians: "His intent was that now, through the church, the manifold wisdom of God should be made known . . . according to his eternal purpose which he accomplished in Christ Jesus our Lord" (3:10–11).

The primary mission of the church—the reason Jesus established it—is to make disciples, to bring people to Jesus Christ, who is the only way of restoring people's broken relationship with the Father. The church is fulfilling its mission when disciples are making disciples. The church is therefore both the result of God's mission being achieved and his means for accomplishing it.

Ephesians mentions two other missions of the church. One is to build up one another. In Ephesians 4:12–13 Paul tells why certain roles of leadership were given by Christ to the church: "To prepare God's people for works of service, so that the body of Christ may be built up until we all reach unity in the faith and in the knowledge of the Son of God and become mature, attaining to the whole measure of the fullness of Christ." Then in verse 16 he says that "from [Christ] the whole body, joined and held together by every supporting ligament, grows and builds itself up in love, as each part does its work." Each believer is responsible to help other believers in the growing process, each person with his or her own gifts.

Edification is a necessary function of the church, but it is not an end in itself—it is a means to the end of making disciples. It is also clear by the Great Commission that the making of disciples implies nurture and teaching. The focus is not just on dunking sinners, but on bringing the world into a growing relationship with the Father through Christ—to be committed followers of Christ, responsible members of the family, and devoted ambassadors of God in his growing kingdom. How does this happen? Not haphazardly or through undirected programs. Intentional disciple making on many different levels is needed.

Making disciples involves much more than making people knowledgeable about faith—it involves "teaching them to obey everything [Jesus] has commanded" (Matt. 28:20). People often recite this part of the Great Commission as "teaching them everything I have commanded you." This has been referred to as "the Great Omission." *Obey* is one of the great four-letter words of our time. But when we ignore obedience in the making of disciples, we leave out what brings people into a life-changing relationship with Jesus as Lord of life. Why do so many church members seem uncommitted to Christ? Why do so many continue to rule their own lives rather than submitting to Jesus' lordship? One significant reason is a lack of day-by-day discipleship in many American churches.

Obedience certainly begins when a person accepts Jesus as Lord and Savior. To place one's eternal life into the hands of Jesus without placing his or her everyday life in his hands is an eternal oxymoron. At the same time, obedience is something one continues to learn. And so nurture is important as the growing disciple learns to obey all the Lord has commanded. This happens only as the Christian becomes more Christ-dependent by the Spirit's power, more in step with the Spirit and out of step with the world (Gal. 5:16–25).

The church that is making disciples and teaching them to obey all the Lord has commanded is a church that glorifies God (Eph. 3:21). Jesus makes this clear in several passages: "Let your light shine before men, that they may see your good deeds and praise your Father in heaven" (Matt. 5:16); "This is to my Father's glory, that you bear much fruit, showing yourselves to be my disciples" (John 15:8); "I have brought you glory on earth by completing the work you gave me to do" (John 17:4). In each of these cases the *mission* has to do with making disciples, and the *result* is that God is glorified.

What Functions and Forms Fit This Purpose?

The New Testament is clear about the purpose of the church, and it demonstrates many of its functions. But it says little about specific forms.

Before looking at forms, however, we need to discuss an important method: gathering and scattering. Jesus demonstrated this method first when he gathered (called) his disciples and then when he selected twelve to be apostles, which means "one sent out." Mark 3:14 illustrates Jesus' method: "He appointed twelve—designating them apostles—that they might *be with him* and that he might *send them out* to preach" (emphasis added). Their mission was not just to be learners (disciples), but eventually to be sent to the multitudes with the gospel. The early church followed this pattern as well. They gathered (Acts 1:4–8, 12–14; 2:1–4, 42–47; and many other instances), and they scattered (Acts 5:42; 8:1–4; and throughout the Book of Acts). Gathering to worship, to be instructed and equipped, to be encouraged, and to encourage are essential elements of Christian living. But these must never become the primary objectives of the church—they are only the means to the end of proclaiming the gospel (scattering). To be the incarnation of the Father—to be Christ's ambassadors—means getting outside the walls of the church building. It means modeling Christ and living for him as the church is scattered in the neighborhoods, in the schools, at the workplaces, in prisons, in hospitals, on the ball fields, in the gyms—making the most of every opportunity (see Eph. 5:16).

Although the word *congregation* is widely used today to designate a local church, the body is better described as a community. Christians are often good at congregating but not that good at living in community with one another. The world sees the church congregating and detects little purpose in that activity. Many people in America today say the church is irrelevant to their needs. At the same time, today's society yearns for deeper relationships—for community.

The early church was that kind of community. On the Day of Pentecost about three thousand people were added to the church. How were all these people assimilated? How were they taught? In community. Acts 2:42–47 demonstrates that community, particularly verses 46 and 47:

> Every day they continued to meet together in the temple courts. They broke bread in their homes and ate together with glad and sincere hearts, praising God and enjoying the favor of all the people. And the Lord added to their number daily those who were being saved.

This new church ministered to one another. They "spur[red] one another on toward love and good deeds" (Heb. 10:24). They loved each other, confessed their sins to one another, served one another, and carried each other's burdens. It is difficult to imagine them "congregating," sitting in rows looking at the back of one another's heads. There was structure and form to the early church, but that structure allowed, even expedited, people to minister to one another as they gathered.

What did that structure look like? Primarily, the first-century church met in the temple courts (large group) and from house to house (small groups). The New Testament is full of examples, particularly in Acts (2:46; 5:42; 20:20). When the writers of the New Testament use the word *church* they normally refer to either a group that met in someone's home (for instance, Philem. 2; Rom. 16:5) or to an entire community of believers in a particular city (for instance, 1 Cor. 1:2; Revelation 2).

The contemporary church need not copy the first-century church's structure to be faithful and fruitful. Each function must fit the church's mission, however, and then the forms (structure) must follow those mission-determined functions.

Where do small groups and Sunday school fit? Individual programs and groups may have specific goals: to build strong relationships in the context of community, to equip people with Bible knowledge so they can serve one another and be a witness in the world, to support one another with specific needs, to recover from some addiction or other problem, to evangelize, to worship, to pray, and so forth. All of these functions are not ends in themselves, however. Each group—Sunday school class, fellowship group, support group, or whatever—must understand how it relates to and has influence on the specific mission of the church: to make disciples.

2

Breaking Down the Walls of Churchianity

Why has the church not continued to explode, as it did in the first century, in discipling all nations? At least one reason seems evident: traditionalism. Churches that are failing today are those that hold on to human traditions—those that are in a business-as-usual mode.

In some churches this relates directly to the Sunday school. The purpose for this program has been lost over the years. Many churches have a Sunday school program because they've always had a Sunday school program. In some churches, small groups systems have already become institutionalized. They may have been started because the successful church down the street had them or a church growth guru recommended them. In either case there is no undergirding purpose for the programs. They plod along with little direction or cause. They are going nowhere, and so are the people involved in them. People today, especially baby boomers and busters, are dissatisfied with this kind of mediocrity in the church.

George Barna's research reveals that the unchurched find the church irrelevant to the way they live. "We currently develop churches based on a model of ministry that was developed several hundred years ago, rejecting the fact that the society for which that model was designed no longer exists," says

Barna.[1] Growing churches, however, have their fingers on the pulse of today's world and are ready to meet the needs of people in the contemporary society.

Can Yesterday's Forms Meet Today's Needs?

Over the centuries many have worked to restore biblical principles to the church. Yet today some church forms are still not designed to help believers practice the "one anothers" of the New Testament. The intimate fellowship displayed in the Book of Acts is missing in many congregations. In many churches the Great Commission—the marching orders from our Lord—remains a job to be done by someone else.

The fields are still ripe for harvest (John 4:35). Yet some harvesters are using yesterday's tools and methods to try to reap it, and they are coming out of the fields empty-handed because of programs that are no longer effective. Worse yet, many harvesters are content with past harvests and are not even going into the fields. The Lord of the harvest has continually provided resources to bring in the harvest. The church must consider how well it is doing as steward of the gospel.

Picking ears of corn by hand may have been an effective means of harvest one hundred years ago, but today that would be considered ineffective work and poor stewardship. Many churches, however, are using yesterday's methods to do God's work today—without success. Some church forms may be yesterday's tools. Some tools need sharpening or fixing. The criterion is the fruit of the harvest.

Notice that the question I'm asking in this section is not, Can yesterday's *functions* meet today's needs? Biblical *functions* come from God and are enduring components of the church. *Forms* are man-made and are fluid and changeable. This distinction is essential to this discussion.

As we consider the places of the Sunday school and small groups in today's church, we must be able to see beyond these forms themselves and look at the functions they can carry out.

Form follows function. Yet churches reproduce traditional forms rather than allowing forms to meet the needs of the particular culture they are trying to reach. Each congregation exists in a particular community that is different from any other community in the country. And yet, across the nation and across the many denominations, most American churches take on basically the same forms and practices.

Why is this? Churches do not intentionally set out to become archaic, of course. Instead, throughout the church's history certain programs and departments, such as Sunday school in the recent past, have been developed to carry out scriptural functions. At the time, these programs were culturally relevant, meaningful to the people, and successful. Then as changes occur in the society, these programs can become irrelevant, meaningless, and unproductive. But they also become traditional, cherished, and in some cases, unchangeable. People often consider them sacred. When this happens, a process sociologists call *institutionalization* happens.

People in the church sometimes see their activities—even those that have very little real spiritual meaning—as means to a biblical end. These activities, which they have done for years in basically the same way, have become so associated with the ends they may have once accomplished that the means have unknowingly become sanctified. They have forgotten the goals of such activities—the goals, in fact, do not matter anymore. Larry Richards asserts in *A New Face for the Church:*

> Somehow church activities have become "holy." A whole pattern of life has grown up centered on *church*. It doesn't matter whether or not church activities guide believers toward maturity. Week after week men and women come into services and go out unchanged—knowing that they have not been changed. And yet they return religiously, week after week, repeating behavior which seems unable to help them toward the spiritual reality they need. Sociologically speaking, an organization which guides members into patterns of behavior which support means without reference to success in reaching goals is a ritualistic organization.
>
> And this *is* today's church.[2]

Jesus made it clear that the church must steer clear of deifying traditional forms, particularly if they do not allow room for authentic growth and discipleship. He spoke boldly to the Pharisees, who asked him why his disciples broke the tradition of the elders. These traditions included meticulous regulations for daily life that were interpretations of the law of Moses. Jesus asked them in return why they broke the command of God for the sake of their tradition. He told them they actually nullified the Word of God for the sake of their tradition and called them hypocrites, quoting Isaiah: "These people honor me with their lips, but their hearts are far from me. They worship me in vain, their teachings are but rules taught by men" (Matt. 15:1–9).

God has given his people creativity to develop and utilize particular tools (such as Sunday school and small groups) for the time in which they carry out the church's witness. But Christians must never forget that these tools are man-made, not God-made. These means should never become untouchable, unchangeable, nonnegotiable. And there should always be room for fresh new ways of carrying out Christ's commission.

"Unwillingness or inability to distinguish between expedients developed a century ago and principles laid down in Scripture is responsible for many of the impediments which prevent us from discipling the world," says church growth specialist Joe Ellis.[3]

Institutionalism describes a good thing gone bad—maintaining the institution becomes the main thing, and that gets in the way, or even negates, accomplishing the primary task of the institution. Joe Ellis writes, "In the church, building an institution sometimes pushes building the Kingdom right out of the picture. The institution then exists primarily for itself."[4] The result, says Larry Richards, is that "the church, rather than guiding believers to become growing Christians, finds itself guiding them to become churchmen."[5]

Personal faith cannot be built with impersonal methods. Spiritual growth is built not by involving people in programs, but rather by encouraging relationships that will support them in their faith.

The New Testament church is built on relationships rather than institutional forms. The way to the Father under the new covenant is through a relationship with Jesus rather than through the old covenant law. Sacrifices, the priesthood, and the tabernacle were all instituted in the Old Testament by Moses, but they passed away with Jesus' coming and by his death on the cross. He and his body, the church, now represent all three Old Testament forms (Rom. 12:1–2—living sacrifice; 1 Peter 2:9 and Hebrews 8—royal priesthood; Hebrews 9 and Eph. 2:21–22—temple of the Holy Spirit). Through the ages, the organized church has tried over and over—and in many ways successfully—to reestablish these three things, thereby turning community into institution. Many churches today have a professional "priesthood," even if those in that position are not called "priests." Some churches see the Lord's Supper and other "sacraments" or rituals in the same manner as the Old Testament sacrifice. Many churches have built huge church buildings that are called "God's house," as if he dwells there rather than in the hearts of Christians. In order to become again a new covenant church, one that meets people's real needs with the everlasting truths of the gospel, church leaders will need to look with a critical eye at their forms and ask if they are driven by relational (new covenant) or by institutionalized (old covenant) means.

Part of the concern over institutionalism is how we view our church buildings. Buildings can exacerbate institutionalism in many ways. For one thing, when the church sees its building as the place where ministry happens, it becomes less flexible. Howard Snyder says that when a church erects a building it cuts down its options 75 percent.[6] Buildings determine programs, budgets, and the number of people who can participate in a worship service or educational programs at the same time. Churches become slaves to brick and mortar in more ways than just financial, rather than being flexible to meet people's real needs.

Our erroneous view of church buildings can also make the church immobile. The Great Commission says "go," but our church buildings say "stay." We are to seek a lost world to redeem it to God, but we often say through our buildings and the services that occur in them, "Let the lost seek the church." If the lost will not "come to church," meaning the church building on Sunday morning, some members feel they must be outside the reach of Christ anyway. But non-Christians often feel intimidated by large, formal church buildings and the services that occur in them. The church's outreach programs are really designed to get people *in*side the church building. There is no evidence of this "come to us" mentality in the New Testament church.

The church's institutionalized view of buildings has been called an "edifice complex." Hadaway, DuBose, and Wright say the church cannot continue to buy land and construct buildings, sheerly from a pragmatic point of view. But they balance the views of others toward the use of church buildings and meeting in homes:

> What is needed is a strategy in which house groups are used both to reach out in new effort and also as a supplement to and/or a combined method with traditional approaches. We are not going to abandon sixteen-hundred years of history of being and doing church in church buildings, despite all the negative aspects of the edifice complex.[7]

The strategy spelled out in chapter 10 demonstrates how to combine a building-centered program and off-campus groups. Before we build such a strategy, however, we need to understand how to break out of an institutionalized mindset regarding buildings and programs.

Breaking Down the Barriers

How can the church move away from institutionalism? In *Church without Walls*, Jim Petersen provides some places to start. He says the church is accustomed to defining itself within a set boundary, which is determined by forms, buildings, and other traditional mind-sets. Everyone knows who belongs and who doesn't belong; what the structure of the leadership is supposed to look like; what members are to believe and, probably more important, what they are *not* to believe; which activities are appropriate and which are not; and what behavior is and isn't appropriate. All of this draws a clear line between insiders and outsiders. Petersen calls this the "bounded set."[8]

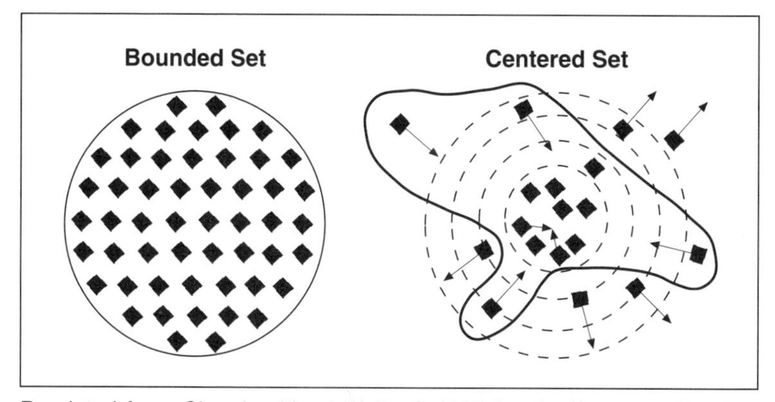

Reprinted from *Church without Walls*. For copies call (800) 366-7788.

Petersen advocates moving from the bounded set to what he calls "centered-set thinking." What is important, he says, is how each person is doing in relation to the center. Belonging is not a matter of performing on some agreed-upon profile, but how one lives and acts out the commitment to the common center. The center is Christ. The focus of the church is pointing people toward the center, regardless of where they are presently. Process is more important in the centered set than definitions.

Petersen's analysis is important. Whatever models for group life are chosen in a church, the ministry will not be effective for long in a bounded-set mentality. To make and continually equip disciples in an effective way will take centered-set thinking. The centered set will be addressed again in chapter 9, in which a strategy for the church will be discussed.

Petersen calls for a paradigm change: "It will mean a reordering of our thinking—away from being centered around sanctuaries, pulpits, pews, and clergy and to focusing on neighborhoods, offices, living rooms, lay people, and our neighbors."[9] He expands upon this theme in *Living Proof* and *Lifestyle Discipleship.*

In *Lifestyle Discipleship,* Petersen addresses one particular paradigm shift that is needed. Often in today's church, he says, people are told, "So you want to follow Christ! Very well. Here are some things you must do. And over here we have another list of things you would do well to give up."[10] The first list might include such activities as worship, Sunday school attendance, and tithing—and if the individual is really going to follow Jesus, attendance on Wednesday night as well. I know of some churches who tell potential members that if they are not in a small group, they're not a part of the church. All of this imposes conformity on people. It focuses on *behavior* instead of a transformation of the heart. We change the label on the same old can, but the contents are still the same. The person may look and act like what we think a Christian is supposed to be, but the changes are outward only and transitory. We have it all backward, says Petersen. Transformation must happen from within, and only God can make that kind of change take place.

The church must face the fact that traditionalism and institutionalism have for years drowned out opportunities to disciple this world for Christ. Before systems can be put in place, before decisions about Sunday school and small groups can be made, before the church can truly glorify God, congregations must bring about a paradigm change.

If some churches do not change their institutionalized ways of thinking, they too may nullify the Word of God for the sake of their traditions.

3

Making Disciples

What is a disciple? In Greek, *disciple* literally means "a learner." Another way to define a disciple is by looking at his or her relationships. A disciple has a dependent relationship with Jesus, an interdependent relationship with other believers, and a redemptive relationship with the world. Perhaps Jesus gave the best definition: "If you hold to my teaching, you are really my disciples" (John 8:31).

Jesus identified two components of discipleship as he called his apostles: "He appointed twelve—designating them apostles—that they might *be with him* and that he might *send them* out to preach" (Mark 3:14, emphasis added). The first part of discipleship is to be with Jesus, to follow him and to grow continually in understanding and obedience. The second part is to be sent—to reach out to others. Here we see the gathering and scattering method of Jesus in action.

Part of being a disciple of Jesus is being obedient to him and to his Word. In the Great Commission, "to obey" is the object of "teaching them." A new believer does not accept Jesus as Savior and then later take him as Lord. The two go hand in hand. Placing oneself under the lordship of Jesus is part of becoming a new creature in Christ.

At the same time, a disciple is a learner. He has not yet achieved Christlikeness—he is working toward it (Phil. 3:12–14). Christians are truly people in process.

The church has redefined discipleship into churchmanship. Living as a disciple takes effort. It means more than just sitting in a pew or a classroom every Sunday morning.

How a Disciple Grows

In 1987 Southeast Christian Church in Louisville, Kentucky, was listed as the sixth fastest-growing church in America. Worship attendance had increased by more than twelve hundred people in one year. The church has continued to grow rapidly, and in 1989–90 was ranked as the twenty-ninth fastest-growing church. In 1992 Southeast had 1,181 additions and its total membership at the end of the year was more than eight thousand. In reference to the growth in 1989, preaching minister Bob Russell said, "But . . . how committed are those 1,200 new people? . . . Do our people really know what they believe? How do we utilize everybody's gifts? How can we shepherd this increasing number of people?"[1]

Charles Swindoll asks a similar question and responds:

> How can a large church that attracts so many people from such varied backgrounds harness the energy and move people from mere spectators to participants? I can assure you it doesn't happen automatically. People don't suddenly get involved, drop their guard, and devote themselves to one another. The secret is a firm commitment to assimilation.
>
> As I realized how easily our church could become a huge body of spectators, strangers to one another and rootless in our commitment to Christ, I began to speak on the value of becoming involved in a small-group ministry—an adult fellowship group, a choir, an evangelistic team, a prayer group, a weekly home Bible class, one of our women's organizations, or men's groups. In any one of these special groups, there could be more in-depth sharing and involvement.[2]

The Great Commission is often called the church's evangelistic mandate. But the stress of those verses is on discipleship. Jesus said to "go and make disciples," not "go and make church members."

That commission indicates the "product" of the disciple-making process: a believer, learner, and follower of Jesus as Savior who is obedient to him as Lord. Disciple making can be pictured like this:

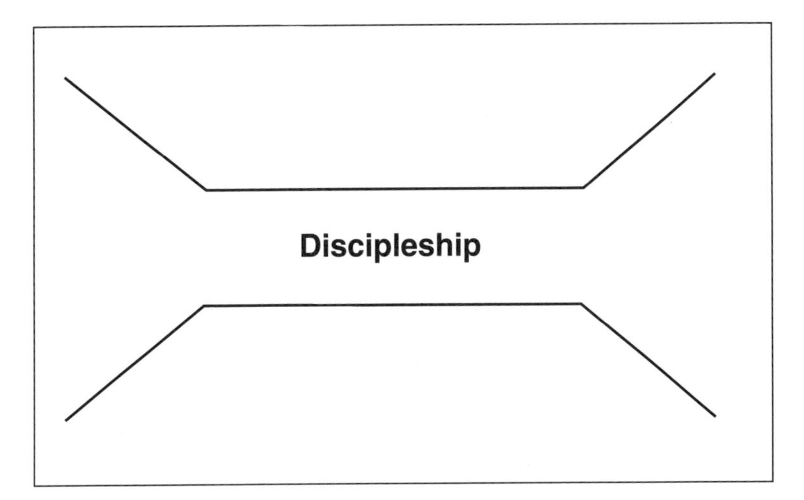

How does this process take place? The individual must establish a relationship with others, including all types of groups. In the group, he is assimilated into the life of the body so that he may begin the disciple-making process. I have found that it is difficult if not impossible to disciple someone who has not been assimilated into a group.

So except for intentionally closed groups (such as support, recovery, or growth groups), every group in the church must work at assimilating and discipling new people. Researchers have consistently found that making new friends in the church is a major factor in retaining new members. Converts who make seven or more new friends normally do not drop out. If transfers do not find a meaningful group within six months, they tend to drop out or become inactive.

One traditional method for assimilating new members is to assign them new-member shepherds. But unless that "shepherd" is a close friend already, this type of programmatic approach may not be very effective. Shepherds and sheep often do not become close enough for any real discipling to take place. Someone does not become a disciple simply by becoming involved in a program.

When my wife, Heidi, and I became members of one church, we were assigned a new-member shepherd, a single man in his seventies. At the time, Heidi and I were in our twenties. Bob (not his real name) had nothing in common with us, had no basis on which to shepherd us, and never spent any time with us. The lack of any real shepherding was not Bob's fault. The shepherding program was not based on real, natural relationships but on an institutional mind-set.

To get people involved—to assimilate them, shepherd them, disciple them—they need to be in a group of people with whom they have some connectedness and who really care for, support, and encourage them.

David Yonggi Cho, pastor of the largest church in the world, Yoido Full Gospel Church, in Seoul, South Korea, says there is practically no back door in his church. "The reason," he says, "is that each home cell group is like a family circle. Through these family circles people feel a sense of belonging, and they are kept in the church."[3]

We cannot assume that people can map out their own discipleship process. Like sheep, they need to be led. But how?

On the Day of Pentecost, three thousand people were added to the number of disciples. Within a short while thousands more were also added. How would the apostles assimilate all these people? Would all these newcomers understand what they were undertaking? Who was going to teach them the basics? How would the twelve shepherd all of them? The enormity of these "problems" for the Jerusalem church was greater than at Southeast Christian Church or the First Evangelical Free Church of Fullerton. The numerical growth was greater, the time span was smaller, and the Jerusalem church had no "organization" set up to assimilate the new people. And perhaps that was to their advantage. Jesus didn't leave a book of instructions for his apostles to build an organization with structures to disciple all the new converts. He gave them his example of discipleship in community. Throughout the Book of Acts, then, the apostles did basically what Jesus did. They met in the temple courts, in the streets, along the roads, and in people's homes—in large gatherings and in small groups. "And the Lord added to their number daily those who were being saved" (2:47).

What a Disciple Does

Disciples grow in community, but they also learn to minister to others in that community. Paul assured the Roman Christians that they were "competent to instruct one another" (Rom. 15:14). To the same "royal priesthood" that Peter addressed in 1 Peter 2:9, he said, "Each one should use whatever gift he has received to serve others" (1 Peter 4:10). The New Testament makes it clear that ministry is to be divided among the whole body of Christ, not just a select few.

In 1 Corinthians 7 Paul repeats the same message three times, that every person should stay in the situation he was in when God called him (vv. 17, 20, 24). The implication is that every new believer is strategically positioned by God. Every disciple has a gift to be used in the body and each has opportunities to utilize that gift in service to others in the community of believers. A role of the church is to help new Christians identify their gifts, to help them find opportunities to serve, and to equip them to use their gifts and opportunities for service *where they are*.

Often, however, the church does just the opposite. New believers get the message that they are to withdraw from old relationships. Many Christians I know in the church have told me they can't witness to non-Christians—because they don't know any. They are so involved in the programs of the church and with their Christian friends that they never seem to have the chance to make new friends with "people they have nothing in common with." This is unfortunate because when we become Christians each of us is in a unique position of influence in the world. No one else has the specific opportunities that we have as ambassadors for Christ. When believers in a church begin to see themselves as insiders in their part of the world—in the office or factory, in the school, in the neighborhood or apartment building, in the family—then the whole body will start working together as it should.

The meta-church model proposed by Carl George is one system that can help people minister where they are. In most churches, staff ministers are burned out from overwork, doing, in effect, the work of the entire body. In the meta-model, ministry is done by the people, in their cell groups and in cell-leader training. This lifts the unnecessary burden off the staff ministers to allow them to do their own specific tasks better. What tasks? "To prepare God's people for works of service" (Eph. 4:12). God has given specific gifts to the leaders of the church to equip the people to minister to one another and move each other toward unity, faith, knowledge, and maturity. The result is that "the body of Christ may be built up." The meta-model allows disciples to make disciples and to care for, encourage, and support one another.

Disciples Are Disciple Makers

Jesus spent most of his time with twelve average men: fishermen, tax collectors, and the like. While he was with them for three years, they were undependable, slow to learn, and at times, self-absorbed. Yet Jesus' plan was to disciple these twelve men and then to turn them loose to take the most important message of all time to the entire world. What if they failed? What was Plan B? There was no other plan. Jesus could have devoted his time to the masses so that they would be saved, but he could not have developed the kind of intimate relationships with them that he had with his apostles. That is the genius of his strategy. By spending time intensely discipling a few, they would be equipped to multiply his message over and over again.

Jesus did spend some time with the multitudes, but he concentrated on the smaller groups, particularly the twelve, and especially the three—Peter, James, and John. After Pentecost the apostles also spent some time with the multitudes, but they spent a considerable amount of time in smaller groups. In years past, the church has stressed reaching out to the multitudes through rallies, revivals, and crusades. Not as much attention has been placed on conserving the harvest, assimilating new members into the body, and helping them to become healthy, growing disciples. This was not the strategy of Jesus or the early church.

The need is to place greater stress on smaller groups of people, but certainly not at the expense of the multitudes. The church must first build the foundation, and that foundation is the small group, just as Jesus' primary ministry was with his small group. Small groups themselves, however, do not make disciples. Neither do Sunday schools, evangelism programs, or worship services. Programs do not make disciples. Disciples make disciples.

At the same time, however, different size groups are the context in which discipling takes place. Several levels of group sizes can be involved in the disciple-making process. In a one-on-one situation one person disciples another, maybe someone he or she has led to Christ. Or it could be between two Christian brothers or sisters who agree to meet for study, prayer, confession, or encouragement. Vulnerability and accountability are also key ingredients in this smallest of small groups. The second level is a group of three or four people, usually the same sex, who meet regularly to pray, study, share, and hold each other accountable. In small groups of eight to twelve, intimate relationships can be built to allow disciple making to take place or to encourage disciples to use their opportunities in the marketplace and in the neighborhoods to make disciples. Sunday school classes may also be utilized in the disciple-making process, especially for Bible learning and application. The larger the size of the class, however—unless the large class is broken down into smaller groups—the less opportunity there is for true discipling to take place.

The Lookout magazine[4] once received a letter from a reader who disagreed with an article about the Great Commission. She argued that Jesus gave the commission to his apostles only, not to Christians today. The thought is absurd! Jesus would not give instructions, especially instructions as important as these, that would be impossible to fulfill. But it would have been impossible for twelve individuals, or even 120, to disciple *all* nations. In fact, the genius of Jesus' strategy is that his commission would be passed on from disciple to disciple to disciple, through the generations, until all the world could be discipled.

Disciples making disciples uses the law of multiplication. In the past the church has used the law of addition. As an example, say an evangelist wins one thousand people per day (a rather good harvest!). At the end of one year he has won 365,000 people. At the end of twenty-five years, he has won 9,125,000 people.

Multiplication works differently and more slowly. Say a disciple wins and trains one person a year. At the end of one year, there are two disciples. But each of those two disciples wins and trains one person the following year, and so on. At the end of twenty-five years, 33,554,432 disciples have been won and taught. It would take the evangelist nearly ninety-two years to win that many people to Christ (without being able to adequately disciple them). Using the multiplication method as described above, the entire world could be discipled in less than thirty-five years.

Only certain individuals in the church have the spiritual gift of evangelism (Eph. 4:11). Peter Wagner says only 10 percent of church members have the gift of evangelism and only $\frac{1}{2}$ percent are doing it.[5] But everyone is a witness. In Acts 1:8 Jesus said, "You will be my witnesses in Jerusalem, and in all Judea and Samaria, and to the ends of the earth." The apostles could be his witnesses in Jerusalem, and maybe Judea and Samaria, but it would have been too much to ask of a few relatively uneducated men to be his witnesses to the ends of the earth. That assignment was given to all Christians, and all who are really his disciples have the ability and opportunity to carry it out either in their own neighborhoods or workplaces or as overseas missionaries.

If God's church is to multiply the way he intended, it must get serious about discipleship.

PART 2
ZOOMING IN

Small Groups *and* Sunday School

4

The Growing Influence of Small Groups

How long have small groups been around? That depends on definition. Some people say the Trinity is actually the first small group! Throughout biblical history, small groups of people met for different reasons. In Exodus 18 Moses, on the advice of his father-in-law, Jethro, broke the people into several levels of group sizes, the smallest of which was ten. Jesus carried out his ministry in a small group, and the first-century church extensively used small groups that met in people's homes to teach the new converts and to reach out to many others (Acts 2:46–47; 5:42; 19:8–9; 20:20; Rom. 16:5; 1 Cor. 16:19; Col. 4:14–15; Philem. 2).

Some writers have identified John Wesley as the first person to bring an organized small group movement into the church. (Others suggest that the use of small groups in the church predates Wesley.) In the eighteenth century he divided his geographically centered societies into "classes," which consisted of twelve people each. These classes were the cornerstone of Wesley's entire organizational structure. They met weekly in homes and were led by either men or women. Such classes were the equivalent of today's fellowship groups or house churches, not instructional classes as the term suggests today. Those who professed assurance in salvation were placed in select groups, called "bands," of five to ten people. All Methodists were members of classes, whereas about 20 percent were in bands. Those in bands who were progressing markedly in holiness were placed into cell groups called "select societies." This organizational structure provided the necessary leadership for all the groups.

Like Sunday school, small groups were first used in parachurch organizations. In the 1950s, covenant-type groups began, particularly on college campuses with emphasis on Bible study. In the 1960s the idealists took over with mission and action groups with an emphasis on social concern. In the 1970s the small group movement began to move into the church. Growth groups and "encounter groups" became popular. Self-fulfillment and support were emphasized. In the 1980s the small group movement and the church growth movement began to join forces. This marriage brought more credibility to the small group movement, and more churches began to start small groups, although at first most of these groups were not considered part of the overall ministry of their congregations. A balance between Bible study, mission, and support became the emphasis of groups.[1] Hopefully, the 1990s will become known as the decade of integration in the church—all types of small groups, Sunday school, and other programs working together in an integrated system to more effectively make and equip disciples.

Involvement in Groups

It's been said that trying to define small groups is like trying to describe the proverbial elephant from close up. What you end up describing depends on what part you're looking at. Involvement in small groups is not easy to gauge, for several reasons. First, it is difficult just to define what a small group is. How small is small? What defines a group? Second, many churches do not keep attendance records for their small groups. Home-based groups are informal; taking attendance can seem to formalize the process. Third, there are many different types of small groups, and the types may not be exactly the same from church to church. Fourth, many small groups still meet basically on their own. The church may recognize that they meet and may even put information about these groups in their bulletins, but they are still independent of church structure. There are also small groups that are independent of any church or denomination and meet in factories and office buildings for lunchtime Bible studies, on high school and college campuses, through sports teams (a small group of Cincinnati Bengals, like many other professional teams, meets regularly for Bible study, prayer, accountability, and support), and through parachurch organizations.

Nonetheless, researchers have tried to get a handle on small group involvement.[2] I have also done research on small groups, and I've found it's like trying to get a handle on Jell-O. As soon as you think you've got it, the thing changes its shape and slides through your fingers. In 1993 George Barna, in magazine articles and in his book *Absolute Confusion,* created controversy and possibly more confusion when he said small groups were getting smaller. He stated that according to his polls the percentage of adults involved in small groups dropped from 25 percent in 1992 to 17 percent in 1993.[3] He went on to tell us, with obvious sarcasm, why "the 'church of tomorrow' is falling apart today."

I have several concerns about Barna's findings.

1. For the reasons stated above, I don't believe research can adequately get a handle on small group involvement.
2. The research itself was flawed. Here is how the question was worded in the January 1992 survey: "Are you currently involved in 'participating in a small group Bible study, fellowship group, or prayer group, other than a Sunday school class'?"[4] Here is how the question was asked in the January 1993 survey: "Are you currently actively involved in 'a small group that meets regularly for Bible study, prayer or Christian fellowship, not

including a Sunday school or 12-step group'?"[5] These are two different questions, the responses to which cannot be accurately compared. The question on the 1993 survey, in fact, is more limiting—it excludes Twelve Step groups and adds the word *actively*—which would easily account for the so-called decline.

3. I doubt the validity of Barna's findings because the findings of others tell a different story. George Gallup and Robert Wuthnow researched small group involvement in a three-year, Lilly Endowment–funded study and found that 40 percent of all Americans are involved in some kind of small group. Their survey is much more broad in scope than Barna's; they include any group that meets regularly and provides caring and support for its members. This could include groups such as Sunday school classes and bowling teams. What is interesting is that these researchers perceive the small group movement to be increasing, not declining. Wuthnow describes the growth of small groups as "a phenomenon that has spread like wildfire in recent years." He says, "the small-group movement has been effecting a quiet revolution in American society. Its success has astounded even many of its leaders. . . . Small groups are not only attracting participants on an unprecedented scale; they are also affecting the ways in which we relate to each other and how we view God. . . . In responding to social and personal needs, this movement has been able to grow enormously."[6]
4. Publishing houses and other small group resource providers have an ever increasing demand for small group materials. More small group trainers and consultants are available today to help churches begin small group systems. It follows, then, that there is an increasing number of small groups, not the opposite.

Other statistics are interesting and perhaps helpful to a church with a small groups system. In his 1992 survey, Barna found that blacks are almost twice as likely as whites to be involved in a small group; lower income people are more likely to be involved; people who live in the Midwest and South are the most likely, while people who live in the Northeast are least likely to be involved; and females are 12 percent more likely to be involved in a group than males. In the survey I conducted, 38 percent of people who attend the church's worship service are involved in a small group (in churches that have small group ministries). *Newsweek* reported that some 15 million Americans are involved in about five hundred thousand support groups.[7]

Benefits of Involvement in a Small Group

Real involvement in the life of the church is low in most congregations. Roberta Hestenes says the church has a "spectator mentality." She compares the church to a football team on which most of the players are content to sit on the bench and cheer on the superstars. Sitting in the locker room listening to lectures and studying game plans does not win games or develop players. Getting onto the field for face-to-face contact in practice builds muscles and insights so that the player can participate with success. This is where small groups come in. Many Christians do not get involved in Christlike living—in being a real disciple of Christ—because they lack face-to-face contact with other Christians who intimately share the love of Christ. "Too often the church exhorts, but it does not train. It preaches but does not equip," says Hestenes. Small groups can help solve this problem. "Among all the varied facets of a church's program, small groups provide a place where questions and doubts can be raised in a supportive environment," she says.[8]

David Yonggi Cho says, "Not everyone can be an elder or deacon in a large church; not everyone can teach Sunday school or provide counseling, but with home cell groups there is an opportunity for everybody to become involved."[9]

Sociological Benefits

Sociologist Charles Horton Cooley (1864–1929) wrote about the need for people to be involved in a group that he says is primary in linking man with his society and in integrating people into the social fabric. By primary groups he says that he means

> those characterized by intimate face-to-face association and cooperation. They are primary in several senses but chiefly in that they are fundamental in forming the social nature and ideals of individuals. The result of intimate association, psychologically, is a certain fusion of individualities in a common whole, so that one's very self, for many purposes at least, is the common life and purpose of the group. Perhaps the simplest way of describing this is by saying it is a "we."[10]

The small group, as I define it, is a primary group. Other primary groups, such as the nuclear and extended family, the secure workplace, and the close-knit neighborhood, are all in a state of disarray today.

Baby boomers and busters, especially, need this primary group that will become like an extended family. Forty percent of busters have gone through their parents' divorce. Churches that can provide the stability and continuity this generation seeks through small groups and other opportunities will reach these individuals with the love and fellowship of those groups and ultimately with the love and fellowship of Christ.

Lewis Coser comments on the importance of the primary group and compares it to other groups. This is especially relevant when put in the perspective of the current condition of the usual Sunday school class:

> The primary group is built upon the diffuse solidarity of its members rather than upon an exchange of specific services or benefits. It is, moreover, a nursery for the development of human warmth and sympathy, which is contrasted to the formal coldness, the impersonality, the emotional distance of other types of relations.[11]

Coser goes on to speak about the emotional growth that occurs in the primary group, but this can be said for spiritual growth as well. In fact, if the word *Christian* is used to replace *human* and *social* in the following statement, this defines a healthy Christian small fellowship, growth, or support group:

> Sensitivity to the thought of others—responsiveness to their attitudes, values, and judgments that is the mark of the mature man according to Cooley—can be cultivated and fostered only in the close and intimate interactions of the primary group. Hence, this group is the cell in which characteristically human growth takes place. In the primary group the immature and self-centered person is slowly attuned to the needs and desires of others and becomes fitted to the give-and-take of mature social life. The primary group fosters the ability to put oneself into the position of others, drawing the individual out of egocentric isolation by building into him that sensitivity to the clues of others without which social life would be impossible. "In these [primary groups] human nature comes into existence. Man does not have it at birth; he cannot acquire it except through fellowship, and it decays in isolation."[12]

It is no wonder that psychologists say many clients improve more quickly in small group therapy than in one-on-one counseling. Individuals in Christian support and recovery groups benefit not only from the mutual support of others but also from the opportunity to become sensitive to the needs of others and to draw themselves out of their own "egocentric isolation." This is not only true of support and recovery groups, however. People in small Bible study and fellowship groups can also receive this kind of care, support, and focus if the group members intentionally build supportive relationships with one another.

Individuals in the church are interdependent, or at least they should be. Each person has been given a spiritual gift, and no one person has all of them. A lone believer, therefore, cannot usually take advantage of the opportunities he has without the help, reinforcement, and encouragement of like-minded brothers and sisters. Together they can do much more than any could alone. This synergy is what makes the small group effective as a group and helps each individual be more productive in his or her own ministries.

Evangelistic Benefits

The synergy of the small group is an especially positive factor in the witness of the group. Evangelism is best when it is a team, not an individual, effort. The various gifts of members allow the group to reach lost people in a way no individual could. When all the members see themselves as witnesses wherever they are—in the offices, factories, neighborhoods, schools, hospitals, stores—the entire group can have a tremendous impact, especially when each member is praying for and encouraging everyone else. When an unbeliever comes to a group meeting and is made to feel welcome, accepted for who she is, cared for, and encouraged, she is meeting Christ, maybe for the first time, through the Christians in the group. As she studies Scripture with the group and comes face-to-face with the person of Jesus, she will fall in love with him. And when she turns her life over to him, she is already assimilated into the body and has a natural shepherding/discipling network. The small group is a natural for reaching out to our lost world.

Many models for evangelism exist in the small group world. Carl George's empty chair (a symbol that the group is always open to newcomers) and apprentice (a person in training to birth a new group at some point) allow for outreach to non-Christians and multiplication of groups. Lyman Coleman's system includes "door ministries": support and recovery groups that meet the real needs of people who are outside the church. Regardless of the model, small groups that keep evangelism as a main focus can help bring searching people to Christ, assimilate them into the life of the church, and help them grow closer to God as disciples as they grow closer to the others in the group.

By their nature Bible study and fellowship groups can easily become inward and cliquish. This is an area that group leaders and church leadership must watch. Covenant groups are generally closed groups—new people are not invited or welcome—whether the group at first intended for it to be closed or not. There is no organized system for multiplication of these groups. Lyman Coleman says these groups rule out evangelism and reaching the uncommitted of the church. "Having started these kinds of groups in the early sixties myself, I now look upon some of those churches as the most dysfunctional churches in America," says Coleman. "Ten years ago they had eighteen groups; they have eighteen groups today. They have never gone anywhere."[13] Roberta Hestenes, who has promoted the covenant model for years, admits that these groups can turn

> inward to find their happiness and satisfaction in each other to the exclusion of outsiders at the avoidance of the costs of true discipleship. The Christian life is not to be lived at the level of navel-gazing. While small groups profitably and usefully deal with the feelings, joys and anxieties of their members, there is a much bigger world outside the group which demands involvement. The group must find its life in the rhythm of withdrawal and involvement, the mixture of the inward and the outward journey; the hungry, the hurting, the lost of the world demand our discipleship.[14]

Many small group specialists now say that some kind of specific system must be in place in the church's groups to foster evangelism. Such a system may include the concept of the open chair and an apprentice. Without such a system, groups close, become cliquish, and do not carry out the Great Commission. Carl George says that with the possible exception of support and recovery groups, "the notion of group members closing themselves off in order to accomplish discipleship is a scourge that will destroy any church's missionary mandate."[15]

Leadership

The keys to effective small groups are strong leadership and training. Leadership is certainly necessary for accountability of small group leaders. But leadership is also required because small group leaders, apprentices, and others need coaching, affirmation, support, encouragement, and advice. Leadership training has many positive effects. One, of course, is the quality of the small group meetings and the care of the people in groups. Another effect, and just as important, is the quality of the church itself. Trained small group leaders easily move into other areas of leadership in the church—in new ministries, departments, and boards. The use of apprentice leaders perpetuates leadership in the church and for the groups, making church growth more possible.

The leadership of the church serves the small group leaders, who in turn are the servants of the group members. This bottom-up leadership should be nothing new to the Christian church in view of Jesus' words and examples (Matt. 20:20–28; 23:11; Luke 22:24–27; Phil. 2:1–11).

In this model the pastor is at the bottom of the inverted pyramid of leadership. He is integral in the system, training coaches to do their job of training leaders or, in smaller churches, training group leaders directly. The pastor manages the system, cheerleads it, promotes it from the pulpit. The people look to him for supervision, but perhaps even more important, they look for his approval. If he is not really involved in the small group system, many members may not deem small groups important.

Every level of leadership between the preaching minister and the group member must be dedicated to serving the level above it. The small group itself should maintain an air of informality—it should not seem programmatic. But the oversight and management of groups should be seen as a program that demands strong leadership and training.

I like Carl George's model for small group leadership. Named the Jethro II model after Moses' father-in-law (Exodus 18), this model provides for one overseer (coach) for every five small groups and an overseer for up to ten coaches. This system makes the group ministry manageable and practical. In smaller churches, a staff minister, perhaps the pastor, can act as the coach, but as the number of groups multiplies—and as the church grows!—laypeople should become coaches. George describes the model more fully in *Prepare Your Church for the Future.*

The Future of Small Groups

"For the past twenty years, progressive churches have been strapping Small Groups onto their traditional structures," says Haydn Shaw. "But the model that actually provides discipleship and numerical growth designs the rest of the church's structure around groups once they are in the center place."[16]

The model Shaw refers to is the meta-church, described in Carl George's *Prepare Your Church for the Future.* This model requires a complete redesign of the church. Whether or not a church decides to implement the meta-model—and there are many reasons not to, including its relegation of the Sunday school as optional or only for "fishing pond" purposes—it would be a mistake to merely add small groups to the church's list of ministries. For them to be effective, small groups need to be integrated into the entire functioning of the church.

The church that integrates small groups into its entire ministry will be what Lyman Coleman calls a church *of* groups, not merely a church *with* groups. That's not to say everything has to happen in a small group, but that the church is built around community, which happens in all sorts and sizes of groups. Small groups cannot meet all the needs of all the members of the congregation. We must never forget that small groups are not the answer to all of the church's problems. Jesus is the answer to our problems. We need to be careful not to deify the form of small groups. As J. Gregory Lawson said in an article for *Christian Education Journal,* "A danger of cell groups is that they may become another form, method, or ritual of the 'institutionalized church,' another 'god' that people follow instead of the true and living God."[17]

Ron Johnson, area director of Church Dynamics Institute, gives three purposes small groups cannot serve:

1. Specific, in-depth teaching that, in traditional churches, the adult Sunday school or electives provide. Johnson suggests using short-term seminars for this kind of teaching.
2. The vital need that people have to be in a larger group. Again, Sunday school provides affinity groups for fellowship. Johnson also suggests that several small groups gather several times a year for fellowships.
3. An entry point within the church that, Johnson says, can be a fishing pond for the small groups. He suggests a new-members' class for this purpose.[18]

So what does the future hold for small groups? Carl George, of course, believes small groups *are* the future for the church. He says his meta-church structure, which includes small groups as its primary organizational unit, "is the system that will dominate numerically flourishing churches of the future. With the promise of superseding every system of care developed to date, the Meta-Church is the most effective way to reach today's harvest and make disciples of Christ."[19]

Robert Wuthnow has similar convictions about the small group movement:

> It is now poised to exercise even greater influence on American society in the next decade than it has in the last two decades. The resources are there: models have been developed, leaders have been trained, national networks have been established, and millions of satisfied participants are ready to enlist their friends and neighbors.[20]

5

Is There a Future for the Sunday School?

Since the end of the last century, Sunday school has been the preeminent institution for adult Bible teaching and, at least in evangelical churches, reaching people for Christ. But it wasn't always that way. In its inception Sunday school was a means to teach children and youth only, and when it was extended to adults, people were suspicious and even condemning of it. Many leaders would not allow Sunday school classes to be taught on church grounds.

In the late 1880s things began to change slowly. An adult class was started at Calvary Baptist Church in Washington, D.C., and by 1889 it was so successful that an adult department was under way.[1] Through the 1960s, Sunday school attendance skyrocketed, and it brought unprecedented growth to many churches. James DeForest Murch called the increased interest in adult Bible schools "the most striking development" of the early twentieth century.[2] He figured that in 1914 fifty thousand adult Bible classes were organized with about 2 million members. Lyman Coleman estimates that by 1950, 75 percent of church members were involved in Sunday school.[3]

The Sunday school movement had many positive effects on the church besides tremendous growth. First, it was led primarily by nonstaff church members, which helped to somewhat blur distinctions between laity and clergy. Second, Sunday schools became the seeds for planting new churches in many areas. Third, Sunday school brought some elements of the New Testament house church fellowship back into the church. Fourth, Sunday school classes provided opportunities for new-unit growth.

In the 1920s through the 1940s, many Sunday schools were larger than the worship attendance at those churches. Sunday school was the main entry point into the church. The focus of Sunday school was outward—evangelism was a primary emphasis. It was not unusual for people to make decisions for Christ during Sunday school classes. In many churches most of the membership came through the Sunday school.[4]

But around 1950 the emphasis of the Sunday school began to change from evangelism to the spiritual nurture of believers. While teaching methods improved during this time period, evangelism was increasingly considered the work of the ministerial staff rather than the teachers of the Sunday school and the students. Evangelistic rallies were in vogue at this time. But this helped fuel the notion that evangelism was an event rather than a lifestyle. Later, especially in Baptist churches, bus programs became a way of reaching people for the Sunday school, and many churches grew as a result. But the rate of growth had slowed from the previous decades, and in the 1970s attendance began to decline.

In *Growth: A New Vision for the Sunday School* Arn, McGavran, and Arn track the decline of the Sunday school during the 1970s and 1980s. They say that the total Sunday school, church school, and Sabbath school enrollment in American churches declined from 40,508,568 in 1970 to 24,600,000 in 1985, a decrease of 40 percent in fifteen years. This occurred while total church membership grew by more than 9 percent.[5] The main reason they give is the change in focus from those outside the church to those inside—from evangelism to nurture. Like other institutions, the Sunday school fell into the trap of abandoning its founding goals to maintain the institution.[6] As the Sunday school declined, the small group movement was beginning to gain momentum.

Sunday School Involvement Today

Before discussing the reasons for the decline in Sunday school, it will be useful to look at who is involved in Sunday school classes today. George Barna researched involvement in Sunday school and provided information that can be useful to Sunday school planners. His results are reported in *What Americans Believe*. Several of his findings prove particularly helpful.

First, the older the respondents, the more likely they are to attend Sunday school. Second, the higher the education and household income, the lower the rate of involvement in Sunday school. This is significant because those who have the most experience with, and who are most likely to support the value of, formal education are the ones *least* likely to be involved in Sunday school. Third, the more urban the community, the less likely the involvement in Sunday school. Fourth, people in the South and Mountain areas are about twice as likely to be in Sunday school as those who live in the Northeast, Midwest, and Pacific areas. This may be attributed partially to education and income levels.

Steve Fortosis cites research that demonstrates five important aspects of Sunday schools today: (1) new members participate more than regular members; (2) older adults and women have a more positive attitude toward Sunday school than younger adults and men; (3) how Sunday school influences the Christian growth of attenders is the most important variable; (4) fellowship is the prime motivator for adult involvement; and (5) the number of years of church membership has little if any influence on an adult's attitude toward Sunday school.[7]

The most significant of these figures are those that point out that the younger adults are, the less likely they are to attend Sunday school. The church must respond to these trends if it is going to reach today's and tomorrow's generations through the Sunday school.

Several writers have commented on the decline of the Sunday school and its apparently dismal future. In 1975 Lyle Schaller said,

> The widely shared impression [is] that the adult Sunday school class will be joining *Collier's*, the ink blotter, the crank-operated telephone, the Philadelphia A's, the convertible, the five-cent package of chewing gum, and the silk stocking as popular elements of American society during the first half of the twentieth century which disappeared during the second half.[8]

Can the Sunday school, like the convertible, make a comeback? Or is it destined for extinction? In 1987 Arn, McGavran, and Arn wrote,

> If the decline in national Sunday School enrollment continues at the rate it has since 1970, in two generations the Sunday School, as we know it, will become extinct! Today, . . . after nearly 200 years as a growing institution, the Sunday School is in serious trouble. . . .
>
> Indeed, the prognosis for the Sunday School, that once great and thriving institution of the American church, may be rapidly approaching "terminal." The question must be asked, "Is there really a future for the Sunday School?"[9]

Before that question can be answered, however, the reasons for the decline of Sunday school attendance must be understood.

Reasons for Decline

There are at least eight reasons for the decline of the Sunday school. They are discussed here as diagnoses. Throughout this section, reference will be made to Elmer Towns's article "The Nine Futures of Sunday School," in which he gives the changes he sees coming about in response to some of the same concerns listed here.

Confusion over Purpose

"Perhaps the major difference between Sunday schools that are growing and Sunday schools that are not growing is their view of purpose," say Arn, McGavran, and Arn.[10] Ironically, in the same book they *illustrate* the problem of not being able to clearly establish the purpose of Sunday school. In chapter 3 they say the purpose of Sunday school is to reach out to unbelievers and win them to Christ. Outward-focused Sunday schools grow while inward-focused Sunday schools do not, they say. In chapter 7, however, the authors maintain that Sunday school should be used to *train* members in evangelism methods.

From a practical standpoint these aims seem counterproductive. If the Sunday school class is going to be a place that is welcoming to seekers, it would be ineffective and insensitive to teach the "how-to" evangelism classes.

Howard Snyder says, "Existing structures need to be examined for their appropriateness for evangelism. Do our structures propel us into ministry or insulate us from it?"[11] Elmer Towns says the Sunday school should not throw in the towel on evangelism. He suggests that Sunday school members network their friends into a Bible study class where they can hear and respond to the Word of God and then be bonded to the church through those relationships made in the class.[12]

Lack of Caring Fellowship

While making disciples needs to be a primary function of most Sunday school classes, this should occur in the setting of community, where people can share their joys and concerns and where the New Testament "one anothers" can be lived.

The Sunday school class cannot normally be as intimate as home-based small groups. Nor does it need to be. Secondary, face-to-face relationships develop well in Sunday school classes of twenty to eighty people. Peter Wagner says when a class grows past eighty, however, participants miss out on fellowship, belonging, and acceptance of new people.[13]

Fellowship starts at this level, but to move to the next level of intimacy, one must be in a smaller group. Primary, heart-to-heart relationships happen best in small groups, but they can also occur in small Sunday school classes or within groups inside Sunday school classes. To bring this about, Sunday school teachers and administrators must make a conscious effort to improve the group life of the class.

"What is missing in the Sunday School is a commitment to the essence and centrality of group life," say Hadaway, DuBose, and Wright. "Often the school is too cognitive in its almost exclusively didactic setting."[14] This has come about, says Carl George, because Christian education directors have been trained to be instructors in academics rather than supervisors of group life. Therefore, Sunday school classes rarely become care units. Instead, he says, "leaders lecture, spoon-feed, and entertain 'listeners' in bigger-is-better classes." Curriculum houses add to the problem, he says, by thinking of their products as "curriculum for formal learning rather than handbooks for activity directors."[15]

Howard Keeley says he tried to get his Sunday school class to be more open and transparent. Finally, one woman opened up and expressed some doubts she had. The other class members gasped audibly and tried to reassure her that she didn't really feel that way. They rejected her honesty and communicated that it was better to keep one's doubts to oneself. Keeley says he rebuked the class and confirmed the woman for being honest and open. He pointed out to them that if they didn't know her true needs, they couldn't really help her. "We need to do everything we can to create an atmosphere of transparency, freedom, and acceptance in all our church meetings and personal relationships," says Keeley.[16]

Is this true? Must all church activities be marked with transparency in relationships? Or is there a place for anonymity in some settings, particularly in Sunday school? Probably the Sunday school teacher is the best person to answer that question for his or her own class. While a certain level of transparency is something to work toward, not all classes may be ready for it. Acceptance, however, can be a mark of every class.

The important thing is that people are cared for in the Sunday school class. Many people who attend Sunday school do not attend small groups because Sunday school is more convenient (free, on-site child care, for instance) or because they find the anonymity of a larger group more appealing. They will not receive real caring in large worship service meetings. So where will they be cared for, encouraged, and challenged to deepen their relationship with God and to seek ministries that utilize their gifts? In the Sunday school class. "The biggest danger of this particular group," says Carl George, "is that it desensitizes church leaders, so that they tolerate benign neglect of marginal, peripheral people. This group may even communicate that it represents the best a church can do at meeting the inmost needs of its people."[17]

The effective Sunday school class has both an outward and an inward focus. Unless the people of God are encouraged and strengthened by one another, they cannot adequately reach out to others with the love of God. Also, the class that really is a care unit will assimilate new members much more easily than one that is cold, stiff, and sterile.

While the typical Sunday school is still more pedagogical than andragogical, Towns says the "Sunday school is changing from an instructional center to a shepherding center."[18] If he is correct, and if it is changing back to a disciple-making center as well, the future of the Sunday school is much brighter than some have suspected.

Low Quality

In his research about what Americans believe about the church, George Barna asked churched adults who call themselves Christians how they would rate nine different aspects of the church (excellent, good, average, or poor). The area that received the second lowest rating was "quality of teaching in the classes and other educational settings" (the lowest rating was for teen programs). Only 28 percent of all adult respondents said the educational ministry of the church is "excellent." The higher the education and household income of the respondents, the lower the percentage of "excellent" scores. Fifty-five- to sixty-four-year-olds had the highest opinion of the teaching ministry (48 percent rated it "excellent"), while eighteen- to twenty-five-year-olds and those sixty-five and older gave it the lowest rating (in each group, 24 percent rated it "excellent").[19]

Many teachers still believe that a Sunday school quarterly or a Bible study booklet is the only training they need. If any other institution allowed its teachers to put in such inadequate preparation, it would likely not be around long. But in one of the most important educational settings in the world—the one that teaches God's Word—such inadequacy is tolerated. Baby boomers, particularly, seek excellence in whatever they are involved in. Many boomers and busters work with top-quality equipment on their jobs; they watch Hollywood-style multimedia presentations in their meetings; they receive training from top educators in their fields at resorts. They are used to the best.

For the Sunday school to begin growing in today's world, teaching must be marked with excellence. This does not mean turning exclusively to professional teachers or spending large sums of money for the best equipment, but it does mean the church must emphasize training and provide top-quality resources whenever possible. That training should not only emphasize the scholastic, however, it must also stress how to care for the people.

Lack of Growth in Students

Paul Benjamin calls the Sunday school a "rather strange school. . . . organized higgledy-piggledly." Strangest of all, he says, is that this is a school from which no one ever graduates. But the purpose of Christian education is supposed to be to produce teachers of others (2 Tim. 2:2; Heb. 5:12). Benjamin says that often when a church member is asked to teach, the reply is "I'm sorry, but I don't feel I know enough to teach a class." Many of those people have up to eight thousand hours of class time in Sunday school and other educational services of the church.[20]

Benjamin observes that the Uniform Lesson Series has been effective in increasing the Bible knowledge of church members, but "the whole process often becomes study for the sake of study rather than study for the sake of ministry."[21] He compares the situation with that of the scribes and Pharisees in Jesus' day. They had knowledge of Scripture but often misapplied it. They were excellent students of Scripture but missed the point of loving and serving others.

In order for the church to restore the "priesthood of all believers" principle, members must be growing to maturity and learning to use their spiritual gifts in ministry. I agree with Peter Wagner in that a priority of the Christian education program ought to be to enable all adults, within one year of their conversion or sometime before the twenty-fifth birthday of second-generation Christians, to know and be able to use their spiritual gifts.

But believers are not equipped for the ministry opportunities they have in their everyday lives. Christians are present in the marketplace, in their neighborhoods, in all the institutions of society where people are hurting. Those are great opportunities to serve those needy people with the love of Christ. But most people would say they are not equipped to do so. Small groups and worship services cannot totally equip believers to serve in the world—Sunday school must fill the gap. Can it do this with traditional methods? Possibly not. This is where short-term electives could help.

Elmer Towns says Sunday school *has* shifted its teaching emphasis from ontology to functionalism.[22] For this reason the Uniform Lesson Series has begun to lose its popularity as more and more classes are using short-term lesson topics.[23] This seems to be a positive trend, especially for baby boomers and busters, who want relevant, practical studies that they can put into practice right away.

The main purpose of the church is to make disciples. That means more than making converts or teaching Bible knowledge, although these functions are certainly primary concerns. It means teaching people to obey Christ, to live like him, and to serve him.

Institutionalism

Today's adult—especially the baby boomer—is not anti-institutional. He believes in the institutions of family, church, government, schools, and business. But he is against any hypocrisy and abuses by institutions. He is more interested in relationships when choosing a Sunday school class than in tradition for tradition's sake or institutions with no apparent purpose or goals.

Organizational charts, enrollment, and class officers mean nothing to most boomers. They look at these formal, institutional methods that were at one time popular as irrelevant to their lives. Since these things are foreign to Scripture anyway, they should not be treated as sacred by leaders if they want to reach people through the Sunday school.

Some things must never change—the Word of God, for instance. Some things must change because of their very nature. Then there are those things that are free to change or to stay the same for a while. A mature Christian can differentiate between what is changeable and what is unchangeable. Sunday school is not sacred—it is changeable. A study of its history demonstrates that. The needs of today's society and today's church should determine the place and the form of the adult Sunday school.

Lack of Space

Part of institutionalism is being tied to a building for all church happenings—the "edifice complex." Sunday school is almost always dependent on building space. Growth creates "good" problems, forcing the church to build or look for other options. Several churches that were studied for this book have run out of building space for adult Sunday school, often because the expanding children's ministry needs the space. At Mason (Ohio) Church of Christ, four of the adult classes meet at Mason Christian Village, a retirement center about a half mile from the church building. But they still have space problems, so they are considering having one class meet at a popular local restaurant.

Churches will continue to face space problems in the future, especially in urban areas. Also, congregations will increasingly need to consider stewardship concerns regarding building programs. The church needs innovative ways to program Christian education, taking classes out into the neighborhoods and back to the homes. In that way the church will really be reaching *out* to the people where they are. Some Sunday schools are already doing this.

Lack of Involvement

The traditional view of Sunday school is that of people sitting in rows looking at the back of the heads of people in front of them, listening to a teacher lecture. Today, more classes are using interaction as part of the Sunday school experience. Discussion is becoming more prevalent in Sunday school classrooms. Baby boomers seek Bible study more than Bible teaching, says Elmer Towns. They want to be involved in the process rather than just listening. They want more than doctrine and theory. They want the lesson to show them how to live—how to apply the Bible to their everyday lives. They want to experience their faith in the midst of Bible study.

Many churchgoers already take a spectator approach to their faith. Sitting and listening to a sermon on Sunday morning has become the expression of many people's Christian obligation. A pedagogical Sunday school model only affirms in their minds that this kind of behavior is acceptable. The responsibility for learning in many classrooms rests solely on the teacher and thereby robs adults of the opportunity to learn God's truths for themselves.

Towns says the role of the teacher needs to be modified to that of a leader and shepherd. He leads the sheep (as a role model), feeds the sheep (through instruction), and tends the sheep (as a protector).[24] "The difference between mediocrity and success in Sunday school teaching is involvement of the student in the learning process," says Towns.[25] Part of being involved in the learning process is the ability to make choices.

Lack of Choices

Research shows that choices are important in adult education.[26] But many churches prescribe what curricula is used in adult classes. Individuals rarely have many choices in what they are learning. Numerous churches now use electives, either in combination with adult Sunday school classes—on Sunday morning, Sunday evening, or on a weeknight—or in place of traditional adult Sunday school.

The church's increased use of electives is particularly advisable since many people today have highly functional needs in education. Boomers and busters especially want practical, hands-on, skill-building classes: how to balance their budgets, how to improve their marriages, how to raise their children, how to discern and utilize their spiritual gifts, how to break bad habits, how to be a witness at work, and so forth. Some Sunday school classes offer such studies, but if all classes major on such topical issues, where will adults get systematic Bible study? It has been shown that adults today lack a basic knowledge of the Scriptures. A balance is needed, and many churches are searching for ways to provide both systematic Bible study and electives.

The Future of the Sunday School

Some established churches have decided to abandon their failing Sunday school programs in favor of small groups. Some new churches are beginning with no traditional Sunday school, but they do have electives. Some church leaders have travelled all the way to Korea to study the largest church in the world, Yoido Full Gospel Church. They return and implement Cho's temple courts and house-to-house model, which does not include adult Sunday school. But that model has been misunderstood. Cho's church has no Sunday school because there is no strong tradition of Sunday school in that culture. It is not a conflict between small groups and Sunday school. As proof, some of the largest Baptist churches in Korea have both small groups and adult Sunday school.

Many churches say they will never give up Sunday school; it has completely different objectives and meets different needs than do small groups. To them Sunday school is still the primary program for spiritual growth in individuals and numerical growth in the church.

Does Sunday school have a future in the church of the twenty-first century? That depends in large part on the willingness of churches to make necessary changes in their programs to reach and teach people in the contemporary culture.

6

Sunday School and Small Groups Side by Side

Here's the bottom line. Which ministry is more effective: Sunday school or small groups? Which carries out the various functions of the church better? Of course, things are not that simple, but it will help us to compare the two ministries and evaluate how each fits into the life of today's church.

We'll start with a general comparison between Sunday school and small groups. The descriptions are certainly not true in every church; in fact, for many factors the word *usually* must be used because of the wide differentiations among congregations.

Comparison of Sunday School and Small Groups

Factor	*Sunday School*	*Small Groups*
Size	10 to 400	3 to 12
Place	Church building, usually	Depends on type of group. Support, recovery, and growth groups usually meet at church building. Fellowship/Bible study groups usually meet in members' homes.

Factor	*Sunday School*	*Small Groups*
Time	Usually Sunday morning	Group decides
Length of time	45 to 90 minutes	90 to 120 minutes
Duration	Open-ended	Usually closed-ended (5 weeks to 3 years)
Dress	Usually "Sunday best"	Casual
Format	Lesson	Discussion
Leader	Teacher	Facilitator
Discussion	Usually conceptual	Personal
Bible study	Usually travelogue	Guided tour
Curriculum	Quarterly, shorter studies, or topical studies	Varies—usually group decides
Focus	Content oriented: information and learning	Process oriented: depends on type of group; relationships important
Purpose	Christian education/training	Group decides
Contact	Back of people's heads when set up in rows; usually surface level	Face-to-face and heart-to-heart
Tone of meetings	Friendly, formal	Friendly, intimate, informal
Level of group life	Designed to create sense of belonging and identity	Designed to foster intimacy and accountability
Homogeneity	Somewhat homogeneous (more than celebration-size group), but	Very homogeneous, particularly in terms of needs, lifestyles, ages,

Factor	*Sunday School*	*Small Groups*
	inclusive of variety of people	generally heterogeneous in sex, race, background
General benefits	Convenience for schedule, child care usually provided, systematic study of Bible	Encourages intimacy, accountability, and high degree of involvement

Historical Comparison

We can also compare Sunday school and small groups historically. The similarities are remarkable. Small group ministries started in the United States in much the same way as did the Sunday school in the 1800s. Both started as organized movements in other countries and came to the United States with speculation and debate. Both have been championed by some and bitterly resisted by others. Before the Sunday school movement, established churches had only worship services. All teaching was either part of the sermon or occurred informally in homes. Systematic Bible teaching was a need in search of a solution—and that solution was the Sunday school.

Sunday school is an integral part of the church. When it was first introduced in the church for adults, however, the Sunday school was quite controversial. It was seen as unnecessary by many people and even radical by some. The Sunday school as a ministry of the church was accepted only because of the Sunday school movement. Published materials, sermons from preachers who supported the innovation, and the founding of Sunday school societies eventually persuaded the skeptics.

Today many leaders are concerned about a lack of spiritual nurture in our churches. They are also looking for natural places for people to bring unchurched friends. And there are many other needs that are not being fulfilled in our churches—needs in search of a new solution. And that solution is small groups.

Like the Sunday school movement of the early 1900s, the small group movement is now recognized by many as a viable means of ministry. The main difference is that the Sunday school did not really replace any other structure. But in many churches today small groups are seen as a replacement for the adult Sunday school. Another difference is the level of integration. Sunday school is one program—it is distinct from other programs of the church such as the choir, worship committee, eldership, women's organizations, and so forth. Small group principles, on the other hand, can be integrated into nearly any program. The elders can perform as a small group. The choir can be divided into several small groups.

Statistical Comparisons

In the rest of this chapter I'll compare data for Sunday school programs and small group systems in three different areas: individual involvement, church programming, and relative effectiveness.

Individual Involvement

- Of people who consider themselves Christians, in a typical month 28 percent attend Sunday school and 29 percent are involved in a small Bible study, fellowship, or prayer group other than Sunday school (George Barna, *What Americans Believe*).
- According to descriptions members said applied to their groups, the most common types of groups are: discussion group—60 percent; support group—52 percent; special interest group—45 percent; prayer fellowship group—44 percent; Bible study group—44 percent; Sunday school class—29 percent; women's group—28 percent; self-help group—26 percent; youth group—20 percent; men's group—18 percent; couples' group—17

percent; house church—12 percent; therapy group—12 percent; singles' group—11 percent; anonymous group—9 percent; covenant group—9 percent (Robert Wuthnow, *Sharing the Journey*).

- In a typical week 23 percent of all adults attend some kind of religious education class at the church.
- Forty-nine percent of all adults say they attend a church worship service.
- Forty-six percent of adults who attend worship on a given day also go to a Sunday school class (Barna, *What Americans Believe*).
- The most likely people to be involved in a Sunday school class or small group, to lead a group or class, or to be in church leadership are over fifty years old, black, married, and living in southern, southwestern, mountain, or midwestern states (Barna, *What Americans Believe*).
- Of adults who attend worship on a given Sunday, 33 percent also go to a Sunday school class and 38 percent are involved in a small group (research conducted by author, 1991–92).
- There are about 800,000 adult Sunday school classes in the United States, composed of between 18 and 22 million members. There are about 900,000 Bible study groups, with 15 to 20 million participants. There are about 500,000 self-help groups, made up of 8 to 10 million people (Wuthnow, *Sharing the Journey*).
- Barna Research Group surveyed 1,024 participants in groups to learn how they feel about the size of groups. Each person was asked how many people were in his or her group and how satisfied he or she was with that size. The results are given in the table below.[1] The smaller the group size, the more satisfied people are with the group. The possible reasons for that satisfaction will be discussed in a section on relative effectiveness of small groups and Sunday school.

Satisfaction with Size of Groups

Group Size	*"My group is ideal size."*	*"I'd like to be in a smaller group."*	*"I'd like to be in a larger group."*
10 or fewer	74%	—	23%
11 to 20	54%	34%	6%
21 or more	34%	56%	—

Church Programming

By telephone I surveyed fifty-four of John Vaughan's one hundred Fastest Growing Churches in North America (1989–90)[2] and asked these questions:

1. Do you have an organized small group ministry? If not, do you have any kind of small groups that meet away from the church building on their own?
2. Do you have a traditional adult Sunday school? (By traditional I mean that classes meet on an ongoing basis on Sunday mornings.) If not, do you have any other church education programs that train and equip people in medium-size groups (say fifteen to two hundred people)?

According to the responses I received:

- 59 percent have an organized small group program.
- 87 percent have some kind of small group meeting.
- 74 percent have a traditional adult Sunday school program.
- 100 percent have some kind of adult education program.
- 62 percent have both a traditional adult Sunday school and small groups.
- 37 percent have both a traditional adult Sunday school and an organized small group program.

Sunday school is still the foundational ministry among the nation's fastest-growing churches![3] These findings are significant, especially for churches that want to grow and are considering eliminating adult Sunday school in favor of small groups, following the advice of Carl George, who relegates Sunday school to low-priority status. It seems that Sunday school, when utilized properly and not continued only for the sake of tradition, is one of the key factors in churches that are growing. But it is certainly not the only factor—far from it. The *functions* that occur within the ministry of the Sunday school, not merely the form itself, are the main determinants of these churches' growth and success.

What functions are especially effective in the adult Sunday school that helps churches grow? Evangelism? Assimilation? A place where community is built and friendships made? This question will be answered in part in the next section, as each of the major functions of the church is addressed as a means of comparing Sunday school and small groups.

Relative Effectiveness

I contacted forty-five churches that have a small group ministry and asked respondents to rank from one to ten the effectiveness of Sunday school and small groups in eleven different categories. The average values from all the responses are shown in the graph below.

Relative Effectiveness of Sunday School and Small Groups

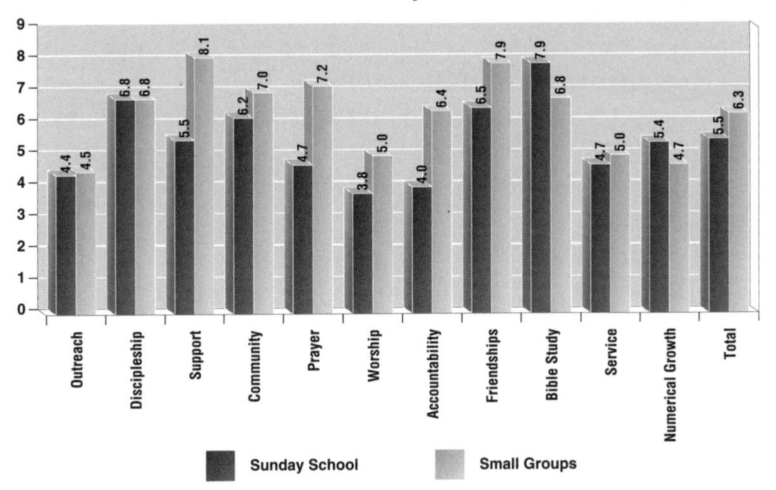

Bible study is the only category in which Sunday school ranked markedly higher in effectiveness than small groups. Judy Hamlin adapted this same chart for her workshop at the National Small Group Conference in March 1992. The participants in the workshop ranked Sunday school and small groups using the same categories, plus one other: assimilation. Their averaged responses brought results similar to those of the survey. Bible study was the only category in which the Sunday school ranked higher than small groups.

What do these findings mean? Two things stand out. First, in categories that deal with relationships, small groups seem more effective overall. The smaller size of small groups, their location, and their level of informality lend themselves to better relationship building. This is no surprise. The findings point to the importance of using small groups to strengthen what have been areas of weakness in the past. Second, the need for Sunday school is reinforced—for the systematic study of the Bible, if for no other reason.

In the following sections, each of the individual categories will be analyzed and compared in more detail.

Outreach and Evangelism

As stated in chapter 5, for most of the twentieth century the Sunday school was primarily outward oriented. In most churches, the Sunday school focused on evangelism. But that began to change in the 1950s and 1960s. Today the main focus of the adult Sunday school is Bible teaching, as the survey shows. In most churches, outreach is at most secondary in importance. Teachers view themselves as instructors more than as evangelists.

The results show that small groups ranked virtually even with the Sunday school in evangelistic outreach. Both scored low: neither ranked higher than five out of ten. Many small groups—especially those in churches that started them in the past two decades—have become closed and ingrown. Their purpose was to build Christian community, and that has happened at the expense of evangelism.

Lyman Coleman, among others, says this has been a mistake. Today many churches are looking at Carl George's model for multiplication of groups and using the empty chair to promote evangelism. And many churches are using small groups to meet people where they are, using support and recovery groups, for instance, as a means of outreach to the community.

A host of Christian education and church growth specialists say that intentionally open groups are now the more effective means of evangelism. Elmer Towns says the church is turning from evangelistic outreach programs (Sunday school busing, visitation programs, and so forth) to evangelistic inreach (side-door or web evangelism—getting to know people in everyday life and inviting them to Bible studies, fellowship groups, and so forth). "Program evangelism has a place and has some results, but such results are small compared to web evangelism," he says.[4]

The Sunday school of the early 1900s reached out through web evangelism. Members of classes invited friends and coworkers to the Sunday school class, where they were welcomed warmly and learned from the Bible. But two things have changed today. First, as already mentioned, the Sunday school has changed. It is more inward focused. Also, the world has changed. Boomers and busters are not as likely to go to the church building as their parents and grandparents were, even when invited. On the other hand, small groups can be more comfortable and less threatening than "school" held in a church classroom and led by a "teacher."

Over the years, evangelism has become a program of the church. Even Sunday school visitation committees may have added to that perception—that evangelism is what a select few of the church do.

The approach of the Sunday school in reaching lost people for Christ is to enroll them in the program. C. Ferris Jordan writes:

> Through planned visitation and outreach programs, the Sunday School reaches out. Every church member should be

> enrolled in Bible study. Special attention should be given to enrolling lost persons. . . . The small number of lost adults enrolled in Sunday School is tragic.[5]

The mission of the church is not to "go and enroll all nations." It is to *disciple* them. Jordan assumes that lost people would, for some reason, *want* to be enrolled in Sunday school classes. Today, at least, door-to-door visitation programs aimed at enrolling the unchurched have little effect, especially when compared to lifestyle evangelism. Jordan says, "Personal evangelism is the task of the Sunday School."[6] No, *personal* evangelism is the task of *persons!* Jordan's philosophy makes evangelism an institutional program rather than an individual response and responsibility.

Robert Coleman says it well:

> This is our problem of methodology today. Well intended ceremonies, programs, organizations . . . of human ingenuity are trying valiantly to do a job that can only be done by men in the power of the Holy Spirit. . . . Unless the personal mission of the Master is vitally incorporated into the policy and fabric of all these plans, the Church can not function as she should.
>
> When will we realize that evangelism is not done by something, but by someone?[7]

Even Elmer Towns, who has in the past encouraged Sunday school enrollment, now says it is not an effective means of evangelistic outreach. "There was a time in the past when enrollment figures were one of the most important statistics in a Sunday school," he says. "Today, many of the major denominations and independent churches have stopped gathering and reporting enrollment figures."[8] He says this has occurred because people's attitudes toward enrollment have changed. People today do not want to make long-term commitments to anything, not even bowling teams, service groups, or hobby clubs. So today churches offer the open hand of fellowship to anyone who visits. They try to make newcomers feel as much a part of the class as every other participant.

David Yonggi Cho says one reason his home cell groups are successful is that "each cell is a nucleus of revival in its neighborhood, because the cell group is where real *life* is found in that neighborhood."[9] Unbelievers become curious, he says, when they see the dynamic faith being portrayed and happy people sharing their faith. They want to know why this group of people is so joyful when all around them there seems to be so much trouble. These groups are "magnets" to non-Christians in their neighborhoods.

A woman who is a member of Cho's church began riding the elevator in her large apartment building, looking for opportunities to meet her neighbors. She asked them if they needed help carrying groceries, held doors open for them, or volunteered help with problems such as stopped-up sinks. Eventually she began a small group and invited the people she had met. She was so successful, says Cho, that today if you visit an apartment building in Seoul on a Saturday morning, you will find cell group leaders riding up and down on elevators, talking to people, helping them, and getting to know them.[10] This goes on naturally, and seeds are being planted for small groups and for the Lord.

These kinds of natural neighborhood outreach opportunities cannot happen in church building–centered Sunday school classes. Also, home groups are infinitely reproducible—there is never the problem of running out of space. But on-site Sunday school classroom space is limited. Small groups can reach more people as they multiply over and over again.

Support and recovery groups are also an effective means of evangelism in today's church. People may not come to the church building for traditional services and programs, but they will come for special events (such as one-day events with special speakers) and to small groups that meet for support in or recovery from certain kinds of felt needs. Many church members have friends, coworkers, family members, and neighbors who would attend a special event or support or recovery group for divorced people, adult children of alcoholics, codependents, parents of children with learning disabilities, stay-at-home moms, and others. Many of these people have never attended church services because they thought they would feel uncomfortable or unwelcome or because they did not think the church could meet their needs. People in today's society are crying out for help and for relationships. The church can respond with the only real help and hope—the love, forgiveness, and healing of Jesus.

Both the Sunday school and small groups need to be intentional about evangelism. It is the first priority of Christ's church. It seems that small groups can be a more natural medium for evangelism, but Sunday school can also provide a middle ground where people can move into a larger group and be involved in more systematic Bible study. In the Sunday school, if it is done properly, people can be assimilated at another level into the life of the church and be equipped with the Word to minister to others who are seeking a place to belong.

Discipleship and Spiritual Growth

Evangelism is only the first step in what the church and the individual Christian are called to: disciple making. Being a disciple and making disciples are not solo endeavors. Individual disciples are to live and serve in the midst of community with a high dependence on brothers and sisters in the Lord. Sunday school classes and small groups act as the communities and the context in which disciples live, learn, care, and serve.

In the survey, the Sunday school and small groups tied in their rankings for discipleship and spiritual growth. Both are important for different reasons.

Disciples are learners. They are constantly in a learning and maturing process. The goal of that process is change toward faith and Christlikeness. Several factors are involved in bringing about this kind of change and maturity in an individual. One is through the experiences of the Christian life and the Christian faith. This experience happens in small groups, where struggles, victories, pains, and recoveries are shared. Another factor for bringing about spiritual transformation is Bible study. Scripture grounds believers in their faith and provides a lamp for their feet and a light for their path (Ps. 119:105). A systematic study of Scripture can occur in the adult Sunday school class.

Where do Sunday school and small groups fit into disciple making? Sunday school can play a major role in helping to incorporate people into the life of the church. Friendships are key to assimilating people, and Sunday school classes are built on webs of friendships. Sunday school classes also provide a sense of belonging that is so important. Sunday school gives people an opportunity to be involved in a task of the church, and this helps them feel more a part of the body. And Sunday school is a place to shepherd people.

"Small groups lend themselves perfectly to growth in discipleship because people learn best when they are part of a caring and committed community," says Jeffrey Arnold. "That is, they grow in understanding and obedience when: they experience things together with other learners; they are held accountable to one another for continued growth; they are affirmed and loved; they are part of a structure that allows for and reaffirms growth."[11]

Finding one's spiritual gift is an important element of discipleship—it is part of maturing in the Christian faith. Arnold says small groups allow people to explore and discover their gifts better than in a larger, more structured, institutional meeting. He says a Sunday school class usually has a main teacher and a few other specific roles. But there is little room for others to find expression for their gifts. In a well-planned and structured atmosphere, most people do not see how their contribution can make a difference. It may seem like there is no job in the Sunday school class that someone is not already doing. The fact is that usually a few people are doing all the work. In smaller groups, says Arnold, there is more opportunity to be involved and therefore to discover and use one's spiritual gift.[12]

Paul Meier says sometimes a person will join a small group thinking he is a Christian, but after he is in the group a while and observes and experiences the discipleship there, he discovers he didn't really know what real Christianity is all about.[13] Small groups find nominal people in the church, those who have attended services and Sunday school for years but have never become more than attenders. In the small group, they see real Christians living out real Christianity; they experience the love of God in his people.

But not every need can be met through a small group. Sunday school aids in helping newcomers get to know a wider circle of friends and in getting people involved in some ministry of the church.

Discipleship occurs on many levels. Worship services and Sunday school provide a base for spiritual development. Worship of God is necessary for any kind of growth to take place; so is some form of structured Bible study. To that base, the church can add more personalized ministries to disciple people wherever they are in their spiritual journey. Small fellowship/Bible study groups, support groups, recovery groups, and growth groups all have a place in helping individuals wherever they are in their lives and in their faith. Even smaller accountability groups can also be added to help growing Christians mature even more in their faith. And one-on-one discipling is often effective both with new believers, to help them mature in their new life, and with more mature Christians, who find the intense accountability and support helpful in growing in their relationship with God.

Care and Support

The survey of relative effectiveness of Sunday school and small groups shows that small groups are perceived to be nearly 50 percent more effective than Sunday school in support. Carl George affirms this: "Only on the cell level can people's deeply felt care needs be met. At any larger-size level, needs cannot be covered adequately."[14]

Why is this? First, small groups are in a better position to be aware of people's needs, struggles, stresses, feelings, and victories than in larger groups such as Sunday school classes. Informality is one important consideration. Many factors make a small group more supportive: the fact that a small group generally meets in a home rather than a classroom, and usually in the evening rather than in the morning; the less structured environment of a small group, which allows people to share needs in a more natural manner; the closeness people feel with one another because relationship building is purposefully built into the meeting time; and longer meetings—usually two hours rather than an hour to ninety minutes.

Size, of course, is another important consideration. Sociologist Lewis Coser says,

> In small groups, members typically have a chance to interact directly with one another; once the group exceeds a relatively limited size, such interaction must be mediated through formal arrangements. . . .
>
> The smaller the group, the greater the involvement of its members, for interaction among a few tends to be more intense than interaction among many, if only because of the greater frequency of contact. Inversely, the larger the group, the weaker the participation of its members; chances are high that they will be involved with only a segment of their personalities instead of as whole human beings.[15]

The smaller the group, the more each person has the ability to know everyone else's real needs, beyond the merely superficial. This can be observed in different-size groups when prayer requests are taken, for instance. The typical large Sunday school class shares needs about Aunt Sally's operation, the missionary family in Ecuador, a child's sore throat. Each of these may be legitimate things to pray about, but they are surface-level requests—easy things to talk about and pray for. It is not unusual for people in a small group that has been together for a while to share more intimate concerns: restoration of parent-child or other relationships, help with overeating or depression, confession of a sin, or asking for help with a personal or spiritual struggle.

Members of small groups can help one another with all types of needs. When our car needed repairs and we didn't have the money to have it fixed a few years ago, members of our small group gave us the money. Every member of our group has moved in the past year. The other group members not only pitched in with the physical help, they helped organize the moves and made sure everything went smoothly. They even brought the families meals for their first few days in their new home. I know of groups in which a participant has gone through a death in the family or some other tragedy. The group members banded together, not only for emotional support but also to help with any physical needs.

The phrase "one another" appears more than sixty times in the New Testament. These commands are never written for certain "leaders," but for everyone to care for and support their brothers and sisters. This happens naturally in the small group, especially when a purpose of the group is to care for each other.

Building Community and Friendships

Small groups scored higher than the Sunday school in perceived effectiveness in both the building of community and friendships. Many people today, particularly those under forty, join small groups more for the relationships than for Bible study. In our hurried and fragmented world of Walkman stereos, Watchman personal TVs, cellular phones, laptop computers, and other technologies that shut us off from the rest of the world, we yearn for fellowship. Many live far from family. We need to belong. We need to be known and to know others more intimately. We need community.

To develop community, frequent interaction between people is necessary. People need to spend time together and get to know each other well, share with one another, and dig deep into their own lives with each other. They need to seek God's answers to their problems and seek his direction for their lives. This interaction will bring a shared vision and purpose only if people involve themselves in others' lives.

In the last section on support, interaction was stressed as a crucial element. It is just as crucial to building community and making close friends. Interaction occurs best in smaller groups. The larger the group, the less interactive people will be with their entire personalities. Therefore, it is more difficult for a Sunday school class (larger than twenty people) to interact and become as close-knit a community as a small group can.

Many churches are just as hurried and fragmented as the rest of the world. Real, intimate social interaction is infrequent. People "attend church" in rows with one-way communication. They stay for an hour or two for worship and Bible school on Sunday morning and have little if any interaction with the rest of the body during the week. Real community cannot grow in that kind of setting.

Koinonia occurs best in the hospitality of the home. A respondent to the survey from Van Ness Community Church in Fresno, California, says,

> My experience is that you can *never* get a Sunday school class to have the warmth and atmosphere a home group has. First, morning hours don't lead to the "relaxed" feel of evening groups. Second, classrooms are more sterile than even a poorly decorated home atmosphere, and they inhibit the closeness that living rooms promote naturally.

Building *koinonia* has to do with more than just the comfortable, informal, and casual surroundings, however. The home is a family place. And the Christian community is a family. The apostle Paul often used the family as an illustration for the church. "Members" meet at church buildings and in classrooms. "Family" gets together in someone's home. Community is built best where "families" gather.

Prayer

Prayer is usually an integral part of the Sunday school class. So why did small groups rank two and a half points higher than Sunday school in perceived effectiveness? Probably for many of the same reasons small groups scored higher in some of the other relational categories. Support, community, worship, and prayer all go hand in hand. Sharing is usually more intimate and honest in smaller groups. In larger groups, prayer concerns tend to be more general and surface level. The interaction that has been discussed in previous sections, which occurs best in small groups, is a key ingredient to the sharing that happens in prayer. When people have the opportunity to share their whole selves with a small group of like-minded people, they can bring their innermost needs and concerns before the group and before God in prayer.

Worship

Both the Sunday school and small groups scored low in effecting worship (although small groups ranked 1.2 points higher). Many people in the church have been conditioned to think that worship occurs only on Sunday mornings at the church building. The Samaritan woman in John 4 might provide a different perspective. At one time she believed worship could happen only in a specific place (v. 19). Jesus corrected her: "A time is coming and has now come when the true worshipers will worship the Father in spirit and truth, for they are the kind of worshipers the Father seeks" (v. 23). It is not where a person is when she worships—it is where her heart is. The first-century believers worshiped God both in public (the temple courts) and in their homes, where they praised God and enjoyed the favor of all the people (Acts 2:46–47).

Worship is a fundamental part of the Christian experience—without worshiping God, a group cannot meet God together in the fullest sense. The chief end of man is to glorify God—nothing on earth compares to coming into his presence. In a small group this experience can be more intimate than in a larger group. This intimacy and interaction among individuals and between them and God is enriched in a small group of close friends.

Support, accountability, friendship, prayer, and *koinonia* all add a dynamic dimension to worship in the small group. Bible study also augments the value of small group worship and vice versa. Reading a psalm or a passage from books such as Isaiah, Hebrews, or Revelation can bring new spiritual insights into a time of worship. And worship invites fellowship with the Holy Spirit and with one another, which makes Bible study more meaningful, relevant, and life changing.

Accountability

Christians are accountable first to God (Rom. 3:19). But believers are also accountable to one another. The apostle Paul told the Ephesian church to "submit to one another out of reverence for Christ" (Eph. 5:21). He also gave specific instructions of accountability to the church in Thessalonica:

> Encourage one another and build each other up. . . . respect those who work hard among you, who are over you in the Lord and who admonish you. . . . Live in peace with each other. . . . warn those who are idle, encourage the timid, help the weak, be patient with everyone. Make sure that nobody pays back wrong for wrong, but always try to be kind to each other and to everyone else.
>
> 1 Thessalonians 5:11–15

In the survey, small groups ranked 60 percent higher in perceived effectiveness in accountability than Sunday school. Why? Accountability grows as relationships grow in trust and love. Accountability cannot be demanded from people before spiritual and emotional bonding has taken place. These things grow in *koinonia*. Again, it goes back to the level of interaction the people in the group have with one another. The smaller the group, the more intimate the interaction and involvement; and the more intimate the interaction, the more trust, care, support, and love are built into the relationships. When people really trust, care for, support, and love one another, they will risk being held accountable by others, and they will be willing to hold others accountable as well.

Not all groups have accountability as an objective. Beginning groups especially would stress other areas of interaction that are easier but that might build up to eventual accountability. Some of these areas would be participation, confidentiality, support, and fellowship. Support and recovery groups, growth groups, and small, two-to-four-person accountability groups hold accountability as highly important to the dynamics of the group.

I am part of a Promise Keepers group that meets every week. One of the main objectives of this group of men from our Sunday school class is to hold one another accountable to live Christian lives of integrity in our homes, places of work, schools, and at church. When we first started meeting, we knew one another pretty well, but not well enough yet to ask the hard questions of accountability.

After several weeks, however, as we got to know one another in the small group and as we shared our hopes, frustrations, pains, and failures, most of the guys started sharing deep emotions, things they had not shared with anyone else, even their wives. Some confessed sins and sinful lifestyles. This group has helped me so much spiritually and emotionally that I will schedule almost everything else around it. Wives of some of the other guys in the group have approached me separately and told me how much they appreciate the group—they have seen remarkable differences in their husbands' attitudes since we started meeting.

Confidentiality is essential to accountability in the group. What is said in the group stays in the group. If anyone even suspects that something he says may be spread outside the members of the group, he will not share. The importance of confidentiality needs to be stressed at every group meeting, particularly when deep issues are being divulged.

Bible Study

Bible study is the only category in which Sunday school ranked markedly higher in perceived effectiveness than small groups. Sunday school is traditionally the place where adults learn the Scriptures. A systematic study of Scripture is difficult, if not impossible, to do in a small group. The ongoing setting of a Sunday school class provides the environment for systematic study. When the objective is to teach information and help learners apply it to their lives in a broad, sweeping manner, the Sunday school classroom works well. Discussion-based Bible study can be accomplished in smaller classes, with chairs placed in circles, or by breaking down a large class into smaller groups for Bible study, discussion, or certain activities.

Not everyone agrees that Bible study happens best in the classroom, however. Martha Leypoldt points to research that demonstrates that much of the significant learning of adults takes place in small groups. She says that small groups of eight to fifteen people allow every person to contribute and gain the most from the group. "In an accepting atmosphere," she says, "the small group provides the possibility for all group members to be treated as persons of worth."[16] The interaction that is needed to create change in people does not happen as well in larger groups, she says.

Larry Richards says informal settings such as the home are better for learning because they are not viewed as "school," and roles are not strictly defined as "teacher," "student," and "subject matter." Informal settings are viewed more as part of life, not as a time set aside for "learning."[17]

Scripture shows that the fellowship of the Holy Spirit (true *koinonia*) goes hand in hand with Bible study. Without the Spirit, Bible learning is merely an academic endeavor. But Bible study at its best is a spiritual endeavor—without the fellowship of the Spirit, real spiritual transformation cannot take place as a result of Bible study. Jesus told his disciples that the Holy Spirit would come to teach them all things (John 14:26). It is the Spirit who helps believers understand God's Word and makes certain that the believer's teaching of the Word is real, not counterfeit (1 Cor. 2:12; 1 John 2:26–27). When Bible study occurs along with community, support, prayer, worship, and even, in some respects, accountability, it is more enriching and valuable for the participants.

Colossians 3:16 demonstrates that the Bible-teaching function is to be mutually shared by all believers in the church: "Let the word of Christ dwell in you richly as you teach and admonish one another with all wisdom." That verse suggests what can happen in a maturing small group, where each person provides insights into the study and everybody gains from the mutuality of experience and mutuality of responsibility. Small groups at their best are synergistic. That is, the combined effect of the constituent elements is greater than the sum of the individual effects.

At the same time, however, several people in the New Testament are singled out as teachers. One of the spiritual gifts is that of a teacher, and presumably not everyone has that gift. In fact, James warns that "not many . . . should presume to be teachers" (3:1).

In the church there is a place for teaching one another—that is, sharing with, supporting, and admonishing one another in small groups or individually—and for the spiritually gifted teacher to instruct fellow believers in a classroom or from the pulpit. These are different kinds of teaching and different kinds of learning. Churches that have tried to replace the classroom environment for teaching with a small group environment are missing part of the biblical picture. Churches that do not provide members with a place to mutually share insights with one another from experience and from Scripture also are missing part of the biblical teaching.

An important accomplishment of the Reformation was putting God's Word back into the hands of the people. The Catholic church at one time believed only the trained clergy could understand and rightly interpret Scripture—it was dangerous in the hands of the laity.

Some people in Bible-believing churches today try to make a case that small group Bible studies are dangerous because of the possibility of false teaching. Bible study should take place only in controlled situations, in the church building and by trained professionals, they say.

Jeffrey Arnold discusses the problems with this kind of thinking. First, it *overestimates* the value of the trained teacher or preacher. They are human and just as subject to making errors and to sin as others. This is not to downplay the pulpit and teaching ministries. Certainly some people have the particular spiritual gift of teaching. But they need to be seen in balance of the overall educational opportunities of the church. Second, this thinking *underestimates* the role and power of the Holy Spirit, who "specializes in applying the

Word to our lives." Third, this kind of thinking *underestimates* the value of people. People who have God's Word written on their hearts and minds have great power and can do great things for God.[18]

Small group Bible study and Sunday school Bible learning are compatible. They help each other. Sunday school students who are also in small groups bring additional insights and experiences to the classroom. Often small group participants make outstanding Sunday school teachers for students of all ages. Members of small groups who also attend adult Sunday school are generally better grounded in the Scriptures. In their small group meetings, they can keep the study of a Bible passage in context because of their systematic study of Scripture in Sunday school. Members of adult Sunday school classes can get involved in ministry by leading a small group. Bible study in Sunday school and small groups does not need to be an either-or situation. To have both Sunday school and small groups studying God's Word is a win-win situation.

Service/Mission

When the ratings for Sunday school and small groups are added together in each category, some interesting insights are provided:

Outreach/Evangelism	8.9
Discipleship/Spiritual Growth	13.6
Support	13.6
Community	13.2
Prayer	11.9
Worship	8.8
Accountability	10.4
Friendships	14.4
Bible Study	14.7
Service	9.7
Numerical Growth	10.1

All of the outward-focused categories received a combined rating of less than ten. (Evangelism and service are focused toward other people; worship is focused toward God. Prayer is also focused toward God, but because of the sharing element and the fact that some prayer is centered on participants' needs, this area can be categorized as inward focused.)

Should classes and groups downplay inward-oriented functions in favor of those that are outward focused? In most instances the answer is no. While classes and groups should never become totally inward focused to the neglect of service and evangelism, the participants need not be ashamed of their stress on building community, support, and accountability in order to become stronger disciples. Service and mission are meaningless if they do not come out of a growing spiritual maturity of individuals who are each part of the body of Christ. People need to be growing in their faith to be used by God.

The advantage that small groups have over Sunday school classes in service has to do with the *koinonia* that grows there. As people get to know one another more deeply, they can help each other realize and use their spiritual gifts, which naturally leads to service. Also, real mission and service grow out of support, accountability, and prayer—all of which rank higher in effectiveness in the small group. As a small community of people begins to support one another with *agape* love, they will also support the specific areas of ministry of each member. They can hold one another accountable for their respective ministries and utilizing their spiritual gifts. And most important they can pray for one another. Many times small group members, after being together for a while—several months or one or two years—find they have a passion for the same ministry, and they each have gifts that strengthen the group for that service.

Numerical Growth

Numerical growth ranked slightly higher in Sunday school than small groups. A main reason for this is the fact that in many churches small groups are not open to newcomers and are not set up to reproduce themselves. But small groups can, if organized to do so, be infinitely reproducible. The new-unit principle can happen better in small groups for this reason. Eventually, Sunday school programs run out of room. Then the church either needs to build new space (requiring huge expenditures of money and other resources), find new space elsewhere, or give up on growth. But small groups meeting in homes can grow and multiply without any inherent barriers.

To do this, however, small group ministries must be set up to continually birth new groups. Without intentional coaching to reach out, grow, and multiply, groups will usually become closed. Groups naturally focus on nurture; it is more difficult, and sometimes even more painful, to stress outreach and evangelism. The empty chair is one good way to make evangelism more natural in the group. An apprentice in each group helps assure the multiplication process and grows leaders for new groups.

Total Average Effectiveness

On the whole, small groups ranked only eight-tenths of a point higher than the Sunday school in effectiveness of the two ministries. It should be noted that some churches have rather weak small group ministries in which there is little or no growth, and some churches have outstanding Sunday school programs in which adults are coming to the Lord and being led to dynamic spiritual growth.

Is there any value at all in replacing an adult Sunday school with a small group ministry? What would be the drawbacks of such a move? If we decide to utilize small groups as well as Sunday school, how might they work together?

7

Either-Or or Both-And?

God] sets aside the first to establish the second" (Heb. 10:9). The author of Hebrews wrote about the old covenant animal sacrifices being set aside to establish the new covenant of Jesus' sacrifice on the cross. Some people say that today God has set aside the Sunday school in the same manner to establish—or reestablish—small groups. "Out with the old and in with the new," say some enthusiastically.

Is it time to stop resisting the critics of Sunday school and let it go the way of outreach bus ministries and temperance societies? Is it either-or, or both-and? On the survey sent to churches across the United States, I asked staff ministers questions dealing with these concerns.

Utilizing Both

Leaders identified several drawbacks and advantages to churches having both an adult Sunday school program and a small group ministry.

Drawbacks

Van Ness Community Church in Fresno, California, does not have facilities for adult Sunday school. They meet in a rented school building for worship on Sunday morning. Several other surveyed churches either rent buildings for Sunday morning services or do not have the necessary room in the buildings they own. Many churches, including several of those surveyed, have run out of room for Sunday school space. Today churches that are overdependent on buildings are hemming themselves in. Growth becomes dependent on building programs, which depend on money. Many churches have opted out of this no-end struggle and have eliminated the building-centered traditional adult Sunday school.

McLean (Virginia) Bible Church lists two drawbacks to trying to run both programs: (1) the time and commitment to both is difficult and takes away from real spiritual growth, and (2) ongoing Sunday school reduces the number of leaders available for small groups. Knott Avenue Christian Church agrees with the latter assessment. Leaders there say that running both ministries drains the leadership pool. Others disagree, saying that both ministries working together can actually produce more leaders. Glen T. Murphy of Milligan Baptist Church in Basking Ridge, New Jersey, says that since small group leaders and Sunday school teachers have different gifts, they are recruited from different pools of people. Therefore, there is no leadership conflict.

Saddleback Valley Community Church in Mission Viejo, California, writes that there seems to be no value in having both an adult Sunday school program and a small group ministry "except for the sake of tradition. A church should choose one strategy or another." A respondent from Crossroads Christian Church in Lexington, Kentucky (a church that is going to the meta-model and has electives but no traditional Sunday school), says, "There is not much benefit these days besides appeasing those who feel that Sunday school is an institution of God and should not be done away with."

George's meta-church, of course, includes the adult Sunday school as optional rather than foundational. George says it is good for

> social mixers for making acquaintances, attraction points for outsiders, forums for teaching certain academic infor-

> mation, or opportunities to recruit and direct people into cell ministry.
>
> If a church has a strong need to continue its congregation-size meetings, then keep them! But repurpose the group so it doesn't become a dead-end road or an organism with a life of self-satisfaction. Make sure the group is serving some greater purpose, such as feeding people into smaller groups that can enable deeper care.[1]

It is important to point out that George does *not* suggest the church eliminate the Sunday school, as I have heard some people say. He does, however, relegate it to a secondary position behind small groups. He says,

> I affirm all the advantages of our current models of Sunday school, . . . but I anticipate that the wave of the future will bring sweeping changes. . . .
>
> I believe that the care system to supplement and eventually supersede Sunday school in priority will be the lay-pastor-led nurture group.[2]

Advantages

George's Congregation Levels principle comes from Peter Wagner's fourth vital sign of a healthy church: celebration + congregation + cell = church. In a healthy church these three functions are properly balanced.[3] Unlike George, Wagner asserts that the middle-size group is essential. He says, "I think joining a congregation [Sunday school class] ought to be a *membership requirement* for an adult joining a church."[4]

Middle-size groups (including Sunday school, choir, committees, and other organizations) help people feel involved in the life of the church. In this size group they are more than spectators in large celebration services, and they are involved in the work and mission of the church, which generally happens best with more than ten or so people.

Many churches said a benefit to running both ministries is that they have different purposes. Mountain View Presbyterian Church in Marysville, Washington, says small groups are oriented toward pastoral care, and Sunday school is designed to be content oriented. Sunday school is the place to build a biblical foundation for everything else the church does and for individual lives. Even though Knott Avenue Christian Church in Anaheim, California, dropped adult Sunday school in favor of small groups and to make space for children's Sunday school, leaders there give several benefits of having both programs. "Sunday school meets specific needs: Bible study, fellowship, social. Small groups meet other needs: intimacy, support, and discipleship." The respondent from College Hill Presbyterian Church in Cincinnati, Ohio, agrees. He says Sunday school focuses on Christian education whereas the bottom line of small groups is "community-*koinonia*-ministry to one another."

At Menlo Park (California) Presbyterian Church, pastors teach most of the Sunday school classes, which average between 150 and 250 people each. Carla Bjork, who directs the small group program, says the pastors' knowledge and experience offer a rich experience not available in the small groups. And the intimacy and support of small groups cannot be found in Sunday school classes.

Some people are just more naturally geared to a Sunday school setting than to small groups, says Bart Steever at Mt. Washington (Ohio) Church of Christ. Young parents generally like Sunday school better because child care is provided.

Calvary Chapel in Spokane, Washington, started in 1982 without adult Sunday school. Calvary does have some adult education classes, called "Body Life Discipling Classes," that meet on Monday and Wednesday evenings. And there have been small groups from the beginning. Now, Calvary has just started an adult Sunday school, called "People on the Run." Its goal is to reach people who cannot commit to coming to a more intensive Monday or Wednesday evening discipleship class. Leaders say it "hits more people at their area of readiness. Sometimes small groups are too threatening; the

Sunday school program, with its larger number of members, is nonthreatening. It helps bring people along at their level of readiness."

Rocky Mountain Christian Church in Longmont, Colorado, has a similar philosophy. "For some folks, a small group is too threatening and intimate," says Sue Sutherland, director of small group development. "They prefer a classroom situation where they can remain unobtrusive and minimally involved." On the other hand, she says that "small groups are needed for people who desire close relationships and support. Small groups allow everyone to easily participate in discussion of the Bible. They promote more accountability and involvement." She goes on to say, "Both are needed because of the varying needs and personality styles of people. Everyone needs to grow in Christ through personal Bible study. Therefore, by offering both content-oriented and relational-oriented groups, people have the opportunity to choose."

The following table summarizes the drawbacks and benefits of having both a Sunday school program and a small group ministry in the same congregation.

Both Sunday School and Small Groups: Drawbacks and Benefits

Drawbacks	*Benefits*
Lack of space	They serve different purposes: process versus content oriented; *koinonia* versus Christian education
Lack of money for building programs	Convenience of scheduling—Sunday school has child care provided, necessary for both
Time and commitment	More choices
Drains leadership pool (contested)	Each hits people at different areas of readiness and spiritual growth; small groups are too threatening for some
Traditionalism of Sunday school programs	Serves different personality types

Replacing Sunday School with Small Groups

"What benefits or drawbacks do you see in replacing the Sunday school program with small groups?" Of the churches that answered that survey question, 87 percent either said there were drawbacks or found "no benefit" in replacing the adult Sunday school with small groups. Thirty percent cited some benefits in replacing Sunday school with small groups (some churches gave both benefits and drawbacks for the question). Of the churches that found a benefit in replacing the Sunday school with small groups, 33 percent do not have a traditional Sunday school program, and 58 percent also listed some drawbacks in replacing the Sunday school with small groups.

Benefits

Saddleback Valley Community Church lists four benefits of replacing Sunday school with small groups. In small groups: (1) more teaching is accomplished, (2) many more leaders are trained and involved, (3) groups can choose curriculum to meet their needs, and most important, (4) ministry needs of group members are better met.

Crossroads Christian Church gives similar reasons:

> The benefits have primarily to do with the dynamics involved in small groups versus Sunday school. So many valuable things can happen in small groups that cannot in Sunday school. Some of these include: accountability to growth, spiritual disciplines, etc. Relationships with others can be developed. Everyone can minister to everyone if it is accommodated properly. Each has the feeling that he is intimately involving his gift. Retention also becomes much more controllable.

Although the statements from these two churches may have some merit, they do not answer the question as to why Sunday school should be *replaced* by small groups. The fact that small groups are more effective in some things than the Sunday school—which was determined earlier to be generally true—does not necessarily mean the Sunday school is not effective.

Sue Sutherland, of Rocky Mountain Christian Church, points out one big benefit in replacing the Sunday school with small groups. "Small groups can meet in homes and no extra space has to be built and no extra expense invested," she says.

Drawbacks

Many churches listed drawbacks to replacing Sunday school with small groups. Here are some of the comments.

"Some people who enjoy Sunday school's proximity to worship (in time and location) wouldn't be in a small-group-only setup."

"The problem with replacing Bible school is the fact that *here* our small groups are not primarily *content* oriented. We not only have a fairly strong Bible school that averages more than 70 percent of our worship attendance, we offer a full program leading to spiritual maturity. The small group isn't set up to do that."

"Where will the people receive the content-oriented disciplined study? If the groups become 'classes,' only students will attend. If the worship time becomes a giant classroom, unchurched people will not attend."

"Some people would miss formal Bible teaching."

"Fewer options!"

"Awful! Where's the opportunity for solid, Bible-oriented, intensive instruction (without taking so much time for sharing, prayer, worship, etc., as small groups demand)?"

"It would be disastrous. Baptist churches who have done that have reached far less people overall."

"To do away with Sunday school would unplug a major element in the growth process of our people."

Finally, John Vaughan says dropping Sunday school in favor of small groups "may be the biggest mistake of all. . . . If North American churches implemented George's ideas [of minimizing the importance of Sunday school in favor of small groups] it would seriously hamper the work of the kingdom."[5]

Two insights come out of the research presented in the last two chapters. First, small groups are perceived to be somewhat more effective than Sunday school in most categories. Second, most churches think it is not a good idea to replace the Sunday school program in most churches with small groups. At first these findings seem contradictory. But, as stated earlier, just because small groups are perceived to be more effective than Sunday school in most categories does not mean Sunday school cannot be an effective, productive program of the church.

Some people may say that comparing Sunday school and small groups is like comparing apples and oranges anyway. The two ministries have different purposes and can carry out their individual functions to different people, at different times, and in different settings.

I contend that not only is there room in the church for both adult Sunday school and small group ministries, but that when integrated in a congregation, they can work together with synergistic results. Let's look at some ways Sunday school and small groups can work together.

Relationships between Sunday School and Small Groups

The graph below shows four relationships between Sunday school programs and small groups in churches that responded to the survey.

Churches That Have Both

The first column shows that 80 percent of the churches have both a Sunday school program and a small group ministry. The survey was sent only to churches that have small groups, so 20 percent of the surveyed churches do not have a traditional adult Sunday school program. Most of them, however, do have some kind of teaching program.

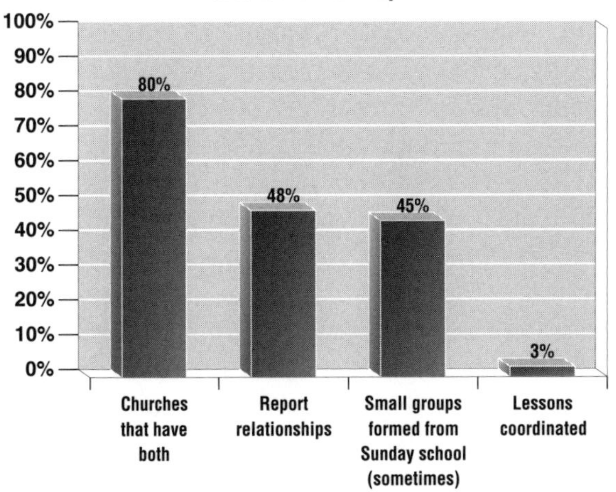

Report Relationships between Them

The second column of the chart shows that 48 percent of surveyed churches that have a traditional adult Sunday school program report some relationship between Sunday school and small groups.

One church that reports a relationship between the two ministries is Ellettsville (Indiana) Christian Church. Some churches view the educational ministry of the church as a banquet—everyone should participate in all the programs. Ellettsville, however, views educational ministries as a buffet—people are encouraged to participate in some kind of educational-discipling group, and every member is expected to be involved in at least one such ministry. Because of people's busy schedules today, Ellettsville does not expect everyone to be involved in both Sunday school and small groups, but they can if they so choose.

Mark Cohea, at Centerville Christian Church near Dayton, Ohio, suggests calling Sunday school classes "small groups that meet on Sunday mornings at the church." Centerville's Sunday school classes usually have fewer than thirty people in each class, and they use a lot of discussion and other small group strategies in classes. Cohea says calling these Sunday school classes "small groups" would "keep a unity of purpose for all groups, and people aren't led to feel guilty for not participating in *two* groups. Some groups meet during the week and some meet on Sunday morning."

Traders Point Christian Church in Indianapolis, Indiana, uses Carl George's meta-church model and Roberta Hestenes's method of transforming committees into communities. In so doing, Traders Point has integrated many of its ministries. But it has gone one step farther. The Sunday school classes have been integrated into the small group system. In a brochure about the small group ministry, Traders Point includes adult Bible school classes. "These classes cover a variety of Biblical issues in a number of different formats," states the brochure. "Most of the classes have also divided out into small groups that meet throughout the week." The primary focus of their adult Bible study classes is to "develop the Biblical literacy of class members through Bible study and application." Traders Point is what Lyman Coleman calls a "church *of* small groups, not merely *with* small groups."

Elmbrook Church, near Milwaukee, Wisconsin, developed several strategies for its small group program before implementing it. One strategy was to coordinate small groups with other church programs. Small groups are officially part of the Christian education program. They have a direct relationship with the adult Sunday school program. Some of the Sunday school classes are organized to train leaders of groups and sometimes to prepare church members to participate in small groups.

Colonial Presbyterian Church in Kansas City, Missouri, developed its small group ministry through its Sunday school classes. Classes function like small congregations within the church, and they provide successful vehicles for beginning new groups and strengthening existing adult classes.[6] David Ruff, pastor of cell groups, said each Sunday school class has a coordinator who promotes small groups in the class, develops new groups from within the class when they are needed, and signs people up for the groups. "They build off each other," says Ruff. "Sunday school becomes a launching pad for small groups and the small groups build the community of the Sunday school."

Small Groups Formed from Sunday School Classes

Of the surveyed churches that have adult Sunday school, 45 percent replied that small groups sometimes form out of Sunday school classes. At Lincoln (Illinois) Christian Church, small groups and Sunday school classes work hand in hand in this way. Sunday school classes are as large as fifty people. Lincoln says it is difficult to shepherd and care for people in that setting. At Richland Hills Church of Christ in Fort Worth, Texas, each Sunday school class chooses small group leaders, and the members of the class then choose which group they want to be in. The Sunday school classes are formed homogeneously, but the groups tend to be even more homogeneous. The survey from First Baptist Church in Atlanta says that "most small groups are formed out of Sunday school classes because some people want a smaller, more intimate meeting during the week."

At Clovernook Christian Church in Cincinnati, Ohio, one Sunday school class averages more than fifty people. The classroom is set up with seven tables with seven to eight people at each table. The same people sit together for an entire series of lessons (usually seven to thirteen weeks). The groups pray together, learn and discuss together, and apply the lesson together each Sunday. Once a month the group that sits together meets in someone's home for fellowship. By the end of the series people have begun to bond in their relationships.

Sunday school classes can incorporate small groups into their structures in at least three ways:

Breakout Groups

Divide the class into small groups of four to ten people (depending on the size of the class) for one part of a lesson. Use breakout groups in any of the following or other creative ways in your adult class.

Prayer—Usually only surface-level prayers are shared in large groups; in smaller groups people feel free to share deeper, more significant concerns. Also, many times those who would not pray aloud in a larger group will in a small group.

Icebreakers—If you could meet anyone from history (besides Jesus—that's too easy), who would it be and why? That's just one example of an icebreaker—an opening question or activity to get everyone talking and to help students know each other on a deeper level. People are more likely to open up about themselves in a smaller group, especially a group in which they know and trust the others.

Activities and discussion—Have breakout groups work on activities or discuss questions. People enjoy working in small teams. Accomplishing something together brings a sense of cohesion between people that is difficult to build in other ways. Modify your lesson plan by breaking into small groups for certain activities to suit your class. Put people together by interests, gender, life stages, or in whatever groupings fit your class and the lesson.

Jigsaw discussion—In this kind of breakout group, each person learns something different and then shares his or her piece of what is being studied with the whole group. Here's one way of doing it. Go around the class and have everyone number off from one to four. Then have class members break out into four-person teams, assigning each team member a number. Give all the groups the same assignment, with four parts that need to be completed. Then have all the ones meet together to do their part together, all the twos meet to do their part, and so forth for all four parts. After these work groups have finished, the teams should reconvene to bring together their separate parts and discuss them.

Breakout groups can be used in many ways, as simple as "neighbor nudges" or reading partners between two people, or as creative as your class is ready for.

Discussion Groups

Discussion groups meet together for an entire class period. They are especially effective in a class that is normally lecture oriented. Set up the room either with round tables or with four to eight chairs arranged in semicircles. A class with discussion groups can be organized two ways. One is to present the entire lesson and then give each group a series of questions to discuss for the remainder of the class. The other way is to break the lesson into three or four sections. After presenting ten minutes of Scripture commentary, for instance, allow the groups to discuss questions based on what was just presented. Either way, it's good to type up discussion questions for each group in advance and have one person in each group facilitate the discussion.

Home Groups

Groups of four to twelve people from a Sunday school class can meet together in members' homes. These groups can study the Bible, pray together, or support one another with specific needs, such as parenting, working through grief, or getting out of debt.

These groups can be an effective outreach tool, particularly if class members organize themselves into groups geographically. Class members invite unchurched neighbors to their homes, where these neighbors can feel more at ease. Later, after they have already met several people from the Sunday school class in the small group setting, the neighbors will more likely respond to an invitation to attend a Sunday school class and other church services.

Home groups can also bring a large Sunday school class closer. The opportunity to build strong relationships, trust, and some accountability will make the adult Sunday school class stronger than it ever could be without this opportunity. Small groups also provide an opportunity for entire families to meet together in one place, whereas on Sunday mornings, parents and children tend to go their separate ways. Even many spouses cannot be together on Sunday mornings, as one or both teach classes or are involved in other ministries.

Whenever a large Sunday school class breaks into smaller groups, good things happen.

Lessons Coordinated between Sunday School and Small Groups

Only one church in my survey reported that lessons are sometimes coordinated between Sunday school classes and small groups. Community Church of Joy in Glendale, California, has elective Sunday morning classes. Sunday school classes are offered on subjects of wide interest. Small groups then "spin off" to deal with the topic on a more personal, in-depth level. Sunday school provides education and some relationship building; small groups have heavy emphasis on building relationships with learning as an added feature. (Many more churches coordinate small group lessons with the pulpit teaching. This follows David Yonggi Cho's house-to-house and temple courts model.)

Prepare Your Sunday School for the Future

What does all this mean to your church? I contend that Sunday school and small groups are a both-and proposition. Research backs up my contention. But I also believe that the present-day adult Sunday school needs to be retooled in most churches. It is failing to accomplish its purposes—if indeed congregations have clearly defined purposes for adult Sunday school classes. Research indicates that many adult Christians are biblically illiterate. And these are the same folks who have been in Sunday school classes for years.

Some writers minimize the place of the Sunday school or suggest it is not really necessary in the church of the future. But a complete change of form may not be necessary—it may even be harmful. Carl George, in particular, suggests a new church structure, called the "Meta-Church." The prefix *meta* means change. While change may be needed, however, the goal of the church is not change. The goal of the church is to make disciples of all nations. That will not happen through one particular ministry, through one system or structure or theory, or through change itself. It will happen when the body learns to work together, utilizing all God has given, including a variety of different ministries and the power of his Spirit.

By saying this, I do not mean that any man-made program is sacred or not expendable. At the same time, I believe God can resurrect even programs that seem dead. He can use forms that some men have given up on. But if the methods themselves are not working, we must work to improve those forms, being good stewards of every tool the church has at its disposal.

PART 3

The Synergy System

8

Traditional Churches in Transition

Dying for Change. Why Nobody Learns Much of Anything at Church: And How to Fix It. Turnaround Churches. The titles of these recent books tell what many people think about the church today. It needs to be changed, fixed, and turned around. And according to George Barna, many are. In his book *Turnaround Churches* Barna comments on his research of declining churches. Some, he says, will inevitably die. Others, though, will be revived, and there are a number of common factors for the turnaround of these churches.

Many churches with programs marked by traditionalism are declining or plateaued. I'm not talking about *traditional* churches—that is, those with traditional programs like adult Sunday school. Traditional*ized* churches are those bound by their programs, those that *cannot* change.

Churches that are willing to change—that even *seek* change—are those that will grow. The adult Sunday school is one place in particular where there must be a willingness to change. "Responding to new situations with flexibility is part of Sunday school heritage," says Simon Dahlman in his editorial in *The Lookout* magazine.[1] He points to the fact that in 1780 the Sunday school promoted literacy among British children, but later, in America, it changed to focus on the Bible. Years after that, most churches began to include adults as well as children. The flexibility of the Sunday school to the changing needs of society and of its individual students has been its strength, and it should continue to be its strength today.

In the previous chapter, I contended that adult Sunday school should not be abandoned in favor of small group ministries, the meta-church, or any other system. However, there are several reasons congregations may choose *not* to have a traditional adult Sunday school.

Newly planted churches, with no traditions to uphold, may find other educational options more favorable to their situations. Another factor to consider is building space. Some churches do not own buildings, and they find adult Sunday school nearly impossible. Small groups along with other training and equipping programs work well for these churches. If the people are maturing in knowledge, love, relationship with others and with God, and in Christlikeness, then the forms in which these things are happening are inconsequential.

Some fast-growing churches with minimal building space may face some of the same considerations. Many churches are growing quickly, and adult classrooms are being—or have been—lost to children's Sunday school classes. Churches across the country face this territorial conflict and are seeking ways to resolve the dilemma. Churches have handled the problem in several different ways. Some have moved Sunday morning classes to other locations such as restaurants or members' homes. Others have moved adult classes to Sunday evenings. Some have even dropped adult Sunday school completely to make space for the children. Which of these options works best? There are no pat answers—it all depends on the situation.

Churches that do have building space available for adult Sunday school still need to consider the best stewardship of that space. Home groups in addition to adult Sunday school can help the congregation become less dependent on the building and less likely to develop an "edifice complex."

There may be good reasons for abandoning the Sunday school in a particular situation, but not because "Carl George says to" or because Cho's church doesn't have Sunday school. The reasons should come from the goals and objectives of the church in addition to the circumstances in that congregation.

One poor reason to continue adult Sunday school is because it is traditional to have one. The Sunday school is a man-made institution and does not transcend culture or time. There may come a time in the church's history when the adult Sunday school becomes unnecessary and expendable, as other structures adopted by the church in its history have. When a church considers the Sunday school imperative and nonexpendable, even when it's ineffective, the structure has become sanctified.

The primary purpose of the church is the making and maturing of disciples, and the programs of the church must be evaluated based on that standard. That may mean the adult Sunday school needs to change in various ways to meet people's needs. It may mean adding new ministries that meet needs better. It will mean different things to every congregation, because the needs in every place are different. One thing seems sure. An unchanging, and especially an unchangeable, program will not be one that is consistently helping people make and mature disciples of Christ. That is not a healthy ministry.

What changes should Sunday school leaders consider? Some of these will be addressed in the next section, but remember, the criterion is how any particular change would help to make disciples and then equip them to be disciple makers.

Sunday School in Transition

A recent book from Elmer Towns is titled *Ten Sunday Schools That Dared to Change: How Churches across America Are Changing Paradigms to Reach a New Generation.*[2] The ten case studies show a variety of ways churches have changed the way they do Sunday school. Each of the situations in these congregations was different, and so were the types of transitions made. In all of these churches, as well as in others I know about, there were six areas of possible change. I use the reporter's questions *why, what, when, where, who,* and *how* to identify these areas. Use these questions to help identify areas of possible change in your program.

Why?

This is the main question, of course. Why have Sunday school? Primarily, the Sunday school is organized to make and equip disciples. How does it do that? Through fellowship, Bible learning and application, support, service, and prayer.

I often hear or read that the adult Sunday school should be the place in the church where people learn the Bible. This becomes a problem when "learning" becomes knowing the facts rather than understanding and living the message. If learning doesn't result in real-life action, changed attitudes, and renewed lives, then our Bible study can end up being like that of the Pharisees. Their objective was to know and practice every minute detail of the Old Testament Scriptures. Yet Jesus told them they were misguided. (Actually, Jesus put it in much stronger words!) They were students—even teachers—of the Scriptures, yet their own lives were unchanged by the message. Their religion was cold and lifeless—even though they memorized the words that bring life. So we must be clear about why we have an adult Sunday school—the purpose for our Christian education—and be certain that vision is shared among teachers.

What?

What is going to be taught? Studies based on the International Lesson Series? Electives? Does each adult class choose its own curriculum based on its needs? Do you provide a number of short-term elective classes that anyone can attend? The answers to these questions should depend in large part on your answer to the first question, *Why?* It should also depend on the needs of the students—what would be relevant to their lives and what format would be most useful to them.

What about the name? The term *Sunday school* has negative connotations for many adults. Besides, as discussed in the next point, Sunday school isn't always on Sundays anymore. *Bible school* is OK, but it still carries negative images of schooldays for some folks. A number of churches are using more user-friendly terms such as *adult Bible fellowship.* Just changing the name can attract people who would not come to "Sunday school." And a name other than *Sunday school* allows for classes to meet on days other than Sundays.

When?

Does Sunday school have to be held on Sunday morning? Not in many contemporary churches. Because of a variety of factors, particularly space problems, congregations are moving adult education from Sunday mornings to Sunday evenings, weekday evenings, and even Saturday mornings. Some churches provide choices of times throughout the week. Lyle Schaller addresses this trend in *The Seven-Day-a-Week Church.*[3] Some have decided to provide Christian education in home-based small groups.

Where?

If your church building were taken away by an act of God, an act of Congress, or even an act of the children's department, would your adult Sunday school cease to exist? If your answer is yes, you have a building-centered program—like most other churches. But remember, adult Sunday school began as a program away from the church building—in rented halls and storefronts. In fact, many people resisted the Sunday school coming into the church building! In America, we tend to think of "church" as a building with stained-glass windows and a white steeple. But really, people are the church!

So here is a question for Christian education ministers and other church leaders: How can the Sunday school be changed to make it less dependent on the building and more centered on people? Here is what a few churches have done.

At Mason (Ohio) Church of Christ, adult classes meet in the retirement center next door. At Knott Avenue Christian Church in Anaheim, California, classes meet at a health club almost three miles away. At other churches, adult classes meet in restaurants, storefronts, trailers, school buildings, rented offices, and homes. There are many possibilities, depending on the circumstances of the congregation. It is usually a lack of space for adult classes, caused by numerical growth, that initiates thoughts of change. But moving off campus with adult classes can be beneficial for other reasons. For several decades Baptist churches began Sunday school classes in storefronts and other places as an evangelistic tool. Could you reach more young adults by meeting over breakfast at a restaurant than in a sterile church classroom? Can you think of other places near your church building where people could meet, not only to free up space in the church building, but also to reach *out* to unbelievers? Or is Sunday school even *for* the unchurched?

Who?

Possibly this fundamental question needs to be answered before some of the above questions. Who is your Sunday school geared for? Is it primarily a training and equipping center for believers, or is it outreach oriented? I do not believe this is usually a both-and proposition. For instance, if I am teaching a class of believers on sharing their faith in the workplace, I have effectively closed that class to unbelievers. I think the Sunday school, because of its usual time and location, should remain open to non-Christians—and members should see it as an opportunity to invite unbelieving friends. Classes on sharing your faith, deepening in spiritual disciplines, and so forth can be electives or special closed small group opportunities.

What age groups do you want to reach through the adult school? Look at your Sunday school today. Is it designed, in format and content, only for people born before 1945? For baby boomers? How about baby busters? Each of these groups may respond better to different teaching methods; and their needs are distinct, so they may be interested in different topics. Offer topics that each of these groups are interested in, and they will come. They will stay if the teaching meets their needs, if the method of teaching helps them learn and keeps them interested, and especially if they make several new friends.

What groups of people do we plan our adult school for? There are the usual groups: singles, young adults, college age, young married, home builders, and so forth. But what about other types of groups? How about classes for people who are divorced? People with addictions? People in blended families? New Christians? The larger the Sunday school the more room for these types of classes.

Men's and women's ministries are extremely popular today, and I believe they are a way the Spirit is moving through the church. How about classes for men and classes for women? That may sound like a regression to previous centuries or to the first-century synagogue, where men and women were separated for teaching. Call me a throwback to a different time, but I think separate men's and women's classes could be a boon to the church, at least if it was one of several other options.

I belong to a couples' Sunday school class as well as a group of men, most of whom attended a Promise Keepers conference. While many of the conversations, discussions, and prayer requests in the couples' class are surface level, even after five years of meeting together, the guys in the men's group, which has met for four weeks now, are already digging deep into each other's lives, holding one another accountable, and really loving one another. Each of us is growing spiritually like we've never done before. We're passionate about our faith. We're excited about sharing it with others.

I've seen the same thing happen with my wife through the group of women that she has joined. For some reason, we can let down our defenses more when we're with a same-sex group. And we've found that men can win other men to Christ and women can win other women more effectively in same-sex groups than through other methods.

There is a time and a place for specialized groups—it may be in your Sunday school and it may not. But you'll never know if you don't ask the questions.

Who will teach Sunday school? Only trained instructors? Do you train teachers in your congregation? Should only elders or shepherds of the congregation be teachers of adult classes, or can anyone who is qualified teach? Can women lead an adult class? Where do your future adult teachers come from? Seeking answers to these and other questions will help leaders make critical decisions about the future of Sunday schools.

How?

What methods work, or don't work, in various adult classes? It's been said that the worst method is the one you use all the time, and there is some truth to that. The question we must ask here, however, is what methods will help adults learn and apply what they're learning most effectively? Are classes discussion or lecture based? Do people sit in rows or in circles? Are classes organized for people to learn individually or interactively? Are classes passive or active? Do adults use several of their senses in a lesson or just one? Answering these and other questions can help adult teachers think about changes that can help them make the learning experience more effective and productive.

Why Nobody Learns Much of Anything at Church: And How to Fix It. The title of this book by Thom and Joani Schultz, published in 1993, tells a sad story about education in our churches. Though the book shamelessly promotes the publisher's curriculum, it does point out some important truths about the state of the church's educational ministry. According to the authors, some of the "problems" with church education today are:

- It has forgotten the goals of education.
- It has a misguided focus on teaching instead of learning.
- It is obsessed with the unimportant.

- It sacrifices thoroughness in order to cover all the material.
- It emphasizes memorization instead of understanding.
- It doesn't promote thinking.
- It prefers passive learning, using lectures and textbooks.[4]

While *Why Nobody Learns Much of Anything at Church* tackles the perceived problems with all church education, many of the authors' assertions are true for adult classes. Here are some of the authors' suggestions for making positive changes:

- Cover less material more thoroughly.
- Communicate what's most important.
- Pursue understanding.
- Ask good questions.
- Allow think time.
- Reduce reliance on memorization and lecture.
- Use active learning.
- Debrief all activities.
- Help learners teach one another interactively.[5]

There are many other *how* questions to consider.

How will we tell others about our Christian education opportunities? There are many creative ways to publicize and market the Sunday school to different groups of people.

How will we group people? Homogeneity may be a great thing to strive for, but what does that mean in your situation? Strictly by age levels, by life circumstances, by interests or needs? Would it help people to mature as disciples if age levels were mixed, or at least if an older couple were to act as shepherds in young adult classes?

How will we decide on a good mix of ongoing classes and electives? How will we reach out to the unchurched in our community through the Sunday school? How will we train teachers? How will we find and recruit teachers of adult classes? How will we assimilate newcomers? Numerous other *how* questions will come up as you begin to decide how to change the Sunday school to meet people's real-life needs. Many of these questions may be easy to answer if a philosophy of ministry has already been formed. Some of these questions may need to be answered even before writing out a philosophy of ministry. Others will need to be hammered out through the process, but the way they are answered should be consistent with your philosophy. In any case, they need to be answered, and those solutions need to be made known to everyone involved in the ministry.

When Transition Goes Wrong

The church should not look for the latest program that will guarantee success, but for a combination of programs that will allow the church to utilize its gifts most effectively. But many churches go from program to program with little if any result. Church leaders travel to Illinois to check out Willow Creek because of its tremendous success, or all the way to Seoul to see what David Yonggi Cho has done to produce the largest church in the world. Many leaders are reading *Prepare Your Church for the Future* and implementing Carl George's metamodel—eliminating the Sunday school or relegating it to relative insignificance. Some of these churches are doing so without weighing out all the factors and consequences. They think implementing the latest fad program will bring automatic success, but as George Barna says, "ministry by mimicry almost invariably results in deterioration rather than growth."[6] Churches should decide on programs based on purposes, goals, and needs, not on conferences and books.

An illustration of how not to implement a program comes from Hoffmantown Baptist Church in Albuquerque, New Mexico.[7] Several staff members went to a seminar held by David Yonggi Cho. They were so fascinated with his concept of home cell groups that they decided to go to Seoul to check out the church and the network of cells for themselves. They were impressed by what they saw, so they decided to implement a program of cell groups at Hoffmantown. They took six months to design a cell group program in conjunction with their existing Sunday school program. Cell groups would provide for discipleship and outreach, and Sunday school would provide teaching and instruction. This amounted to a "radical shift" in the Sunday school.

In 1981 a few cells were started. They grew quickly, and within two years there were about eighty-five groups involving six to eight hundred people a week. At the same time, however, corporate worship attendance began to decline. Some members, particularly older ones, said there was too much emphasis on cell groups.

The church decided to de-emphasize cells and reemphasize the traditional Sunday school program. Small group leaders were reassigned to oversee Sunday school. The structure of cell group oversight was dismantled, and those leaders were given other responsibilities. Groups were allowed to continue if they wanted, but without the support and leadership framework. Within a few months there were only fifty-five groups left, and the church projected that they would dwindle down to about thirty.

Hadaway, DuBose, and Wright give three explanations for the decline. First, implementation of groups was too much too soon. Second, leadership did not adequately communicate the new role of Sunday school to members. Though small groups and Sunday school were to have different functions, that was not communicated to the people. Many members felt the existence of small groups implied the eventual elimination of Sunday school, and so they felt threatened. The pastoral coordinator at the church said, "Where we failed was effectively communicating to the body how the two could fit together." Leaders had told the congregation how cells could reach their city for Christ, but they never gave Sunday school adherents a vision of how they fit into that picture, so they felt abandoned. Third, people more than forty years old never felt ownership of the new idea, and most of them never got into groups. Another big mistake Hoffmantown made was holding their small group leadership training during the Sunday school hour. This told the Sunday school leadership which of the two ministries was most important.

This illustration points to several suggestions for the church that wants to make changes in the adult Sunday school, especially if part of the transition involves implementing small groups:

- Communicate clearly. Clarify goals. Encourage feedback. Respond to feedback, especially when critical.
- Help church members take ownership of the new concept. People need to be involved in the process. Allow input into design and implementation. If members feel like they gave birth to the idea and were involved in putting it into action, they will not feel it was imposed on them.
- Be deliberate. Do not rush into the new venture. As good as growth, evangelism, discipleship, and community seem, without supporting structures and communication systems, growth can actually be harmful to the overall ministry of the church. Just like a new Christian without strong roots, the plant can wither (Matt. 13:5–6). Planning and evaluation are crucial.

In his conference on reaching baby boomers, Elmer Towns gives four suggestions for the church that has both Sunday school and small groups:

> A two-track organization of adult Sunday School and week-day cells can work in the same church. However, (1) do not expect all church members to attend both, (2) communicate the unique purpose of each, (3) give people a choice, and (4) do not project on to cells the resistance some have toward adult Sunday School.[8]

Towns's comments about this two-track system highlight some of the issues involved in integrating small groups and Sunday school into the church's overall programming.

The Necessity of Integrating Programs

There is no one and only "correct" method for making disciples. This is supported in Scripture. In 1 Corinthians 12:4–6, Paul speaks about spiritual gifts, and what he says can be applied to ministries in the church as well as to individual Christians:

> There are different kinds of gifts, but the same Spirit. There are different kinds of service, but the same Lord. There are different kinds of working, but the same God works all of them in all men.

Having a variety of ministries allows people to be involved in the life of the church and to grow at their own level of spiritual maturity, with their own blend of spiritual giftedness. Instead of producing "cookie-cutter Christians," having a variety of ministries allows people to be themselves—the individuals that God made them to be—and to be themselves fully for God.

But just having a variety of ministries is not enough. To be fully effective, those ministries must work together—they need to be integrated.

Clovernook Christian Church in Cincinnati, Ohio, where my wife and I are members, averages about seven hundred people in three worship services. The church has a wide variety of programs: Sunday school, growth groups, recovery groups, and many other groups, committees, and teams. In 1992 Clovernook began FLOCKS—small groups for fellowship and Bible study. The problem, as I saw it, was that these ministries were not related to one another in ways that would be beneficial to the whole church. Most of the groups were seen as independent of one another, doing their own ministries without much correlation to Clovernook's overall purpose and goals. This led to duplicated efforts and missed opportunities.

For example, a member who works with the shepherding program called me one evening to discuss assigning shepherds to two couples in our Sunday school class. I informed him that the couples were already being shepherded in the

Sunday school class. He responded that they had to be assigned new-member shepherds. The problem was that those in charge of the shepherding program and the Sunday school program were not working together so that they would not duplicate efforts. (Finally, the people in the Sunday school class who were already shepherding the two couples officially became new-member shepherds—and then continued to do what they had already been doing.)

Recovery groups, growth (discipleship) groups, and FLOCKS were not connected in any way either. This led to missed opportunities. When a person (sometimes not a member of Clovernook) "graduated" from a recovery group, for instance, he or she would be discipled best if he or she was aware of FLOCKS and other opportunities to help continue the growing process. Or when a FLOCKS group participant seemed to be searching for a greater opportunity for growth and maturity, the leader of that group should have known about growth groups and encouraged that person to get into one. None of these things had been happening at Clovernook.

Some of this began to change, however, in January 1993, when Dick Alexander, senior minister at Clovernook, wrote in the church newsletter about the various care groups in the church:

> It is crucial that every adult at Clovernook be involved in either a Bible school class or a FLOCK. Everybody needs a fellowship group. These groups are the building blocks of the church and are the primary place where love is given and received. It's in a Bible school class or FLOCK that the church is "family." We can do very little to shepherd people who are not involved in one of these kinds of small groups.
>
> If the church is a "hospital," recovery groups are the "emergency room."
>
> . . . Unlike a fellowship group which is an ongoing part of getting through life, a recovery group usually isn't needed forever. . . .
>
> A third kind of small group is a growth group, intended to be a high-protein diet to beef up spiritual life. . . . "Graduates" have the tools for a lifetime of Christian growth. . . .

> The first century church *was* small groups—a major factor in its success. Seven or eight hundred people in our church gathering now on Sunday mornings for worship makes a great community of believers. But people still need a place for closeness and caring.

Many of the churches that responded to the survey are in similar predicaments. They have well-organized programs and groups that do not seem to be connected. Lowell Goetze says a "ministry flow" needs to be developed to help people grow and to continually be challenged in their spiritual maturity. He says "it is a mistake to assume that adult Christians are capable of mapping out their own spiritual growth."[9] A university or seminary would never take such a laissez-faire approach to their students' education. Goetze points out that the Bible calls God's people "sheep," and sheep are meant to be led. He suggests providing a system that provides choices and flexibility, "as well as progression through 'links' or 'bridges' from one ministry to the next." He goes on to state that "without clearly defined bridges from one program to another, people who interrupt their involvement fall between the cracks of various programs." There seems to be no such system in most churches for connecting people with the appropriate programs or groups of the church or for moving people from one group to another to help them continue in their spiritual maturity.

9

The Synergy System

Bible study groups, support groups, evangelistic groups, Sunday school classes, leadership teams, committees . . . by design, all these groups emphasize different things. So what is to keep these groups—and the church as a whole—from going in a hundred different directions?

Purpose. When a clearly defined vision statement is known to all levels of church leadership and membership, programs can be aligned with that mission. Then the programs can be organized and overseen so that they are all working together systematically, cohesively, and synergistically.

The Synergy System is the name I have given a model that can help congregations develop plans for an integrated church of different programs and groups. *Synergy* means cooperative action by different organisms (people or groups) such that the total effect is greater than the effect of the sum of the individual parts working independent of each other. In other words, when two or more groups work together, they can produce more than they all can independently. What that means for us is that the Synergy System is designed to bring together a variety of church ministries in such a way that the overall outcome will be greater than all the ministries could produce individually. This is *not* an easy solution or a cookie-cutter program. It is a cafeteria-style model from which churches can choose the elements that might work best in their situations and circumstances. When these elements work together as different parts of the same body, they should have a synergistic effect.

"The body is a unit, though it is made up of many parts; and though all its parts are many, they form one body" (1 Cor. 12:12). We usually associate the parts of the body with individuals in the church, and that is the correct interpretation according to 1 Corinthians 12:27–31. Another way of looking at these verses, however, is to think of the parts of the body as groups of individuals. For instance, one part of the body is the hand, but it is made up of individual parts such as fingers, a thumb, and a palm. The digestive system consists of many individual parts that make the whole system work. The skeleton is not made up of one long bone but of many, "held together by every supporting ligament" (Eph. 4:16).

In the same way, the church is made up of many different groups of individuals and systems, each of which performs a specific function to keep the whole body functioning as it should. As we put together the Synergy System, we are thinking of a body made up of many *groups* of parts, rather than just the parts themselves. That's not to say that individual persons in the church are not important. They are, of course. But we also want to look at how these individuals are grouped and how these groups work together.

Churches cannot assume members can map out their own spiritual development. That is the role of the church: to provide the ministries and the shepherding to guide people in the development of their faith.

Throughout any church, people are at different levels of spiritual maturity, and they are progressing at their own paces. We can identify at least four stages of spiritual maturity in the church. First, of course, are the preborn, those who are still in the womb of the Spirit waiting to be born again. They require special care and nourishment so that they will be born—and brought into a safe and nourishing environment (John 3:3–8). Those in the second stage are the newborn and young babies. They require gentleness and care, "like a mother caring for her little children" (1 Thess. 2:7). Those in the third stage are the youth, who are growing in knowledge and strength. They need to be treated "as a father deals with his own children, encouraging, comforting, and urging [them] to live lives worthy of God" (1 Thess. 2:11–12). And those in the fourth stage are the mature disciples and disciple makers. They are treated as brothers and sisters who need encouragement to persevere (Gal. 6:9; 2 Thess. 2:15–17; 2 Tim. 3:14) and accountability as role models (1 Thess. 1:4–10).

The goal of all spiritual maturity is to become like Christ (Eph. 5:1; Phil. 2:1–5). At each stage people have different needs and are ready only for what they can bear. Several passages show what should be expected of people at different stages.

> The man without the Spirit does not accept the things that come from the Spirit of God, for they are foolishness to him, and he cannot understand them, because they are spiritually discerned.
>
> 1 Corinthians 2:14

> Like newborn babies, crave pure spiritual milk, so that by it you may grow up in your salvation. . . .
>
> 1 Peter 2:2

> Brothers, I could not address you as spiritual but as worldly—mere infants in Christ. I gave you milk, not solid food, for you were not ready for it.
>
> 1 Corinthians 3:1–2

> We have much to say about this, but it is hard to explain because you are slow to learn. In fact, though by this time you ought to be teachers, you need someone to teach you the elementary truths of God's word all over again. You need milk, not solid food! Anyone who lives on milk, being still an infant, is not acquainted with the teaching about righteousness. But solid food is for the mature, who by constant use have trained themselves to distinguish good from evil.
>
> Hebrews 5:11–14

> Therefore let us leave the elementary teachings about Christ and go on to maturity. . . .
>
> Hebrews 6:1

> Then we will no longer be infants, tossed back and forth by the waves. . . . Instead, speaking the truth in love, we will in all things grow up into him who is the Head. . . .
>
> Ephesians 4:14–15

> Forgetting what is behind and straining toward what is ahead, I press on toward the goal to win the prize for which God has called me heavenward in Christ Jesus. All of us who are mature should take such a view of things. . . .
>
> Philippians 3:13–15

> Consider it pure joy, my brothers, whenever you face trials of many kinds, because you know that the testing of your faith develops perseverance. Perseverance must finish its work so that you may be mature and complete, not lacking anything.
>
> James 1:2–4

Understanding the various levels of maturity in our congregations is important for building a system of ministries that will reach each person where he or she is and help him or her move forward on a path of spiritual maturity and service to others.

Building the Model

The basis of the model is Jesus' method of gathering and scattering. Jesus gathered the twelve and called them *apostles,* which means one "sent out." The apostles' purpose was not just to be learners (disciples), but eventually to be sent out to the multitudes with the gospel. Indeed, they were discipled first by Jesus, but when they were ready, they were sent out to do the work. The early church also gathered (Acts 2:42–47) and scattered (Acts 5:42).

It is Jesus' design for the church to gather and scatter. It gathers to worship, to be instructed, to be equipped, to be encouraged, and to encourage—these are all essential to Christian living, and they must take place in community. But these are only half of what the church is called to do and be. These are the means to the end. The end is to take that equipping and encouragement and scatter to proclaim the gospel. In many churches the means have become the ends. The church is good at gathering. (Even the term *congregation* suggests what the church does best: congregate.) The need is great today for the church—the priesthood of all believers—to begin scattering with the Good News.

I introduced the bounded and centered sets in chapter 2. They illustrate the difference between the church that is gathering only and the church that is gathering and scattering.

The Bounded Set

In the bounded set the church defines itself within a set boundary, which is determined by forms, buildings, and traditional mind-sets. A revised bounded set is shown in figure A (see p. 142). Here, several bounded groups are also shown. These groups may serve effectively in their own spheres, but they have no connection to other groups and ministries. These groups, spinning in their own orbits, represent groups in many churches.

Often these groups are closed cliques. Visitors and those on the fringe of the congregation find it difficult to develop friendships and bond to a group of people in the church, and eventually they are no longer attending church services at all.

In a bounded-set church, and in the groups of such churches, membership is viewed as more important than fellowship, that is, being part of a community (*koinonia*). "Belonging" and social status in the organization are more important than relationships with others and with God. People are often left out of these groups and churches simply because they do not feel like they belong.

People in bounded-set churches and groups act according to norms and "acceptable" patterns. These patterns are easy to define in groups A, B, and C. They define who is in and who is out. Group D is an evangelistic Bible study. The non-Christian is part of the group but cannot find a place in the congregation. Even if there is a group in which non-Christians may feel comfortable and be assimilated into the church, no system exists to help them find it.

How do you know the truly dedicated Christians in your church? "They're at the church building every time the doors are open." That's a typical response in many congregations. But is attendance at meetings a good measure of dedication? More important, is it a good gauge for discipleship? Dedicated disciples of Christ not only seek out the fellowship of other believers at the church building or other places the church meets, they also are out where non-Christians are—they are out in the community ministering to others.

The Centered Set

In the centered set (fig. B, p.143), what is important is how each person is moving in relation to the center, which is Christ.

The primary focus of this church is pointing people toward the common center, regardless of where they are at the present time. The arrows that point out are those Christians who are moving out toward people who do not have a relationship with Christ. The centered set demonstrates the church's strategy of gathering and scattering.

The centered set in figure B is laid over a "target." Lyman Coleman uses this target in his small group seminars to show the three levels of commitment within the church—the dedicated few (10 percent), the pew sitters (30 percent), and the inactives (60 percent)—plus the unchurched community or parish (the door).

According to Coleman 10 percent of the members in an average church are ready for high accountability in growth groups, 30 percent are ready for a covenant (fellowship or Bible study) group, and the 60 percent are not presently ready for any kind of involvement.

How does the church target these audiences? The old way—the bounded-set method—was to aim programs mostly at the dedicated 10 percent and somewhat at the pew-sitting 30 percent. Adult Sunday school has for the most part aimed at these groups of people in the last twenty years or so. But if churches have groups available only for the 10 percent and the 30 percent, they have ruled out the largest part of the congregation, not to mention those unchurched people in the community.

The new science, says Coleman, is to bring people into the church at the "door." These are people of low or no commitment—unchurched baby boomers and busters, for instance. Many of these people who are outside the church can be reached through what Coleman identifies as "door ministries"—support or recovery groups. In the "fringe" zone, low-commitment-level support groups that deal with felt needs will help incorporate the people in this group into the life of the church. Then, the church would move them into the zone labeled "pew sitters." Here they would be in higher commitment covenant groups. The idea is to move people to the center, the "dedicated few," in their spiritual development. Here they are discipled, not just for their own Christian maturity, but to be prepared to scatter—that is, to be sent out to the other zones, particularly to the door to reach others and help bring them in toward maturity in Christ. As this model is put together, other types of groups will be added, especially to the fringe and the door.

Placing Coleman's target on a diagram of a variety of ministries, we have the beginnings of an integrated church model. Figure C (p. 144) synthesizes the gathering and scattering model, Petersen's centered set, Coleman's target, Churches Alive's discipleship model, and my additions and refinements.

The legend at the bottom of the map identifies different groups that could be part of an integrated system. Of course, every church need not include all of the ministries to use this kind of model. In fact, one of the things that George Barna identifies as a characteristic of a turnaround church is that it chooses to do only a few things but do them with excellence. I wholeheartedly agree. Although a wide variety of ministries can help attract a wider variety of people to the church, that will not necessarily happen if most of those ministries are carried out only halfway. Through his research Barna found that a declining church will often try to increase the number of its ministries, even though the congregation may have already been struggling to carry out its present offerings. What is important is that the groups a church has are integrated—connected to one another—in a systematic manner. The open circles in the figure indicate that this is a centered set, not a bounded set—people move through this system freely, and no boundaries hem the church or individuals in to only certain types of activities.

The next phase in bringing together the model is to show individuals who are at different places in their spiritual journeys. In figure D (p. 145) the small dots with arrows illustrate people in the system, both churched and unchurched (a la Jesus' model of gathering and scattering in fig. A and the centered set in fig. C). Some people are moving from one group or ministry to another—either toward the center on their journey of discipleship or out to minister to others. The individual dots with no arrows represent people who are doing nothing—not moving inward on the journey of discipleship or outward in ministry. They are stuck where they are. These dots represent a large number of people in churches. A main purpose of this system is to reduce the number of these inactive, dormant individuals in the church, bringing them into relationships that will help them on their discipleship journey.

But how do these individuals find and move into the most beneficial groups to meet their present spiritual needs? In figure E (p. 146) the transportation system is put into place. The dashed lines represent a system that allows people to move inward on their spiritual journeys, into groups that can aid them in their growth, and outward to minister to others, in groups or individually, at different places in their spiritual walks. These lines also picture the integration of groups. The Sunday school, small groups of all kinds, and other ministries work together synergistically.

Participation in any group is part of a cycle. An individual does not attend a group just to be in that group, but to recover, gain support, grow in knowledge and obedience, learn how to minister to others, and so forth. The objectives of being in a group are to grow in discipleship and to minister to others. When support or recovery groups end, participants should make the transition into a fellowship or covenant group, a Sunday school class, a new-members' class, or a growth group, depending on many circumstances. When people "graduate" from a growth group, they should be ready to take leadership in some other group. For instance, if they have gone through a recovery group, they would be great candidates for starting a new recovery group. Or they may want to get some additional training and lead a Sunday school class. They may want to start a new covenant group or an evangelistic Bible study.

Sunday school classes are the stabilizing force of the system. They are one of the few ministries on the map that are ongoing. People may be involved in a Sunday school class while moving in and out of other groups. They may miss their Sunday school class for a time while being involved in some other Sunday morning activity, such as taking a special elective that will equip for ministry, teaching a new-members' class, or teaching a children's Sunday school class. But they are always part of the Sunday school fellowship to which they belong. This is where their ongoing support, encouragement, and fellowship come from (although they can receive this also in their small groups over a shorter time period).

Evangelism in the Model

Lyman Coleman, Roberta Hestenes, and others see covenant or fellowship groups primarily for Christians. Carl George, on the other hand, sees these groups as opportunities to reach non-Christians. The small groups in this model are designed to reach out. Like the Christian life itself, small groups should be a balance of fellowship and support for those who are Christians and outreach and discipleship for those on their journey to—or back to—God. Coleman says non-Christians are reached primarily through support and recovery groups. But not every unbeliever is interested in, or feels the need to be in, a support or recovery group. What is needed is a multitiered approach to reaching the unchurched. The more entry points the church has, and the wider the variety, the better the opportunity to reach non-Christians in the community. A number of levels can be used to reach people with the gospel. Each of these can be considered entry points for non-Christians.

The size of the church is inconsequential. A small church can start with a couple of groups that have the potential for reaching non-Christians. As they reach more people and begin to grow, they can add on more tiers so that they may continue to reach more people.

First, the church needs to be where people are—not shut up within the walls of the church building, but out in the community, touching people in their everyday situations. In one-on-one situations, Christians can be Christ's ambassadors to bring his healing and hope to people who need them. One of the best ways of bringing people to the Lord and helping them mature as a disciple is in individual discipling situations. This is the first level.

The second level is a web of primary groups such as recovery groups (including Christian Twelve-Step programs), support groups, and evangelistic Bible studies. In addition, new-members' classes at the church building or groups in homes provide opportunities to incorporate people who already have some interest in the gospel or in the church.

The third level is a battery of small fellowship, prayer, Bible study, and task groups, in which people care for, encourage, and support one another on a primary-relationship level. The empty chair is an important part of these groups. Also, the apprentice leader is essential to provide for multiplication of groups.

A fourth level is the Sunday school, where anyone can learn and apply Scripture while developing some primary and secondary relationships with others. The Sunday school class can be an important part of the evangelism strategy when it is an open and accepting place and when the regular attenders are inviting friends and coworkers to join them. The Sunday school is especially helpful in assimilating people into the church because of its proximity in time and place to worship services and other building-centered ministries of the church.

A fifth level is the celebration-size group. Worship services are still an entry point to the church, particularly when they are designed to be sensitive to seekers. They can be a place to which visitors are attracted, where they can hear and respond to the gospel. (I shy away from using the church growth terms *front* and *side doors*. For one thing, these words envision a church building rather than the body of Christ. Also, they conjure up the idea that one "door" is more important, essential, or prominent than another.)

The sixth level is the discipleship or growth group. This is a high-accountability group in which believers aim toward Christlikeness and maturity in their faith with the goal of improving their ability to serve others inside and outside the body. These can be groups as small as two, such as accountability or discipleship partners. While these are not generally places where unbelievers would visit, they are essential in the evangelistic program of the church because disciples are grown here and released for ministry. Growth groups undergird the rest of the levels.

One other level should also be added. Special events such as seminars, athletics, Vacation Bible School, community events, and entertainment events can all be entry points into the church and opportunities to reach people to plant the seeds for spreading the gospel.

An important concept for evangelism in this system is the new-unit principle. The new-unit principle states that just as on a grapevine most of the fruit is produced on new branches, most of the growth in the church occurs in new groups, classes, or churches. Every size church can implement this model because it doesn't matter how many groups a church starts with; what matters is multiplying groups to expand ministry. A small church, for instance, may start with just a few fellowship groups and Sunday school classes, and soon thereafter begin a growth group. Other fellowship groups can be added as leaders become prepared through growth groups, or as apprentices in fellowship groups, and as the groups are ready to multiply. Elective classes, new-members' classes, support and recovery groups, and evangelistic Bible studies can be added to the program to meet the needs of people in the church and in the community as the church grows and leaders are prepared.

It is important to remember that there is no one correct way to organize a system of integrated groups. Each church is unique and each program must reflect that uniqueness. Every congregation must evaluate its own needs and its areas of strength and weakness, and with prayer and dependence on Jesus Christ through the working of the Holy Spirit, set appropriate goals and decide which route to take.

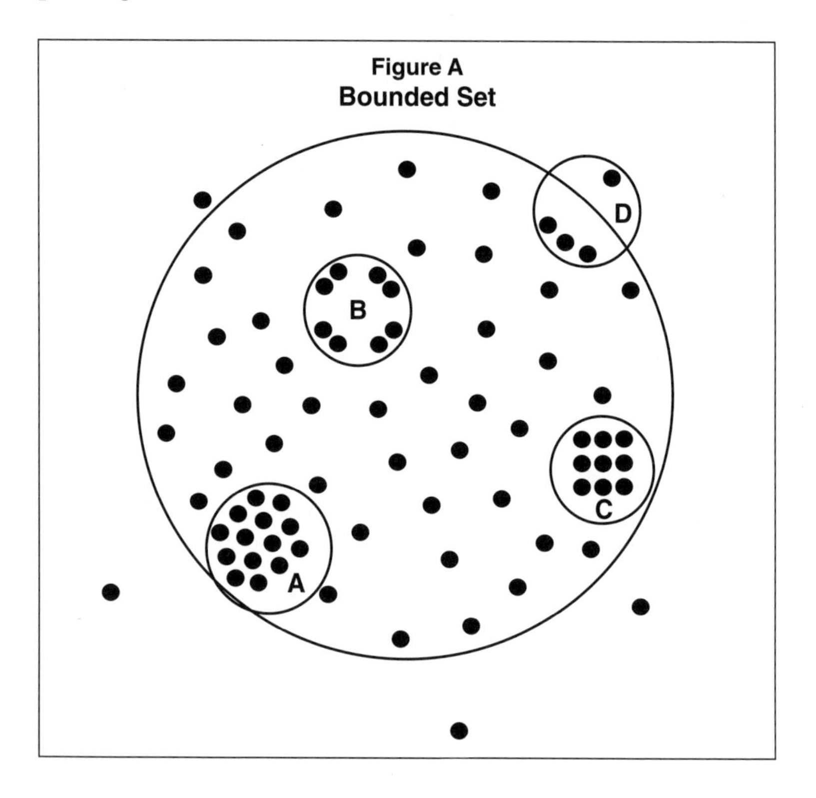

Figure B
Centered Set

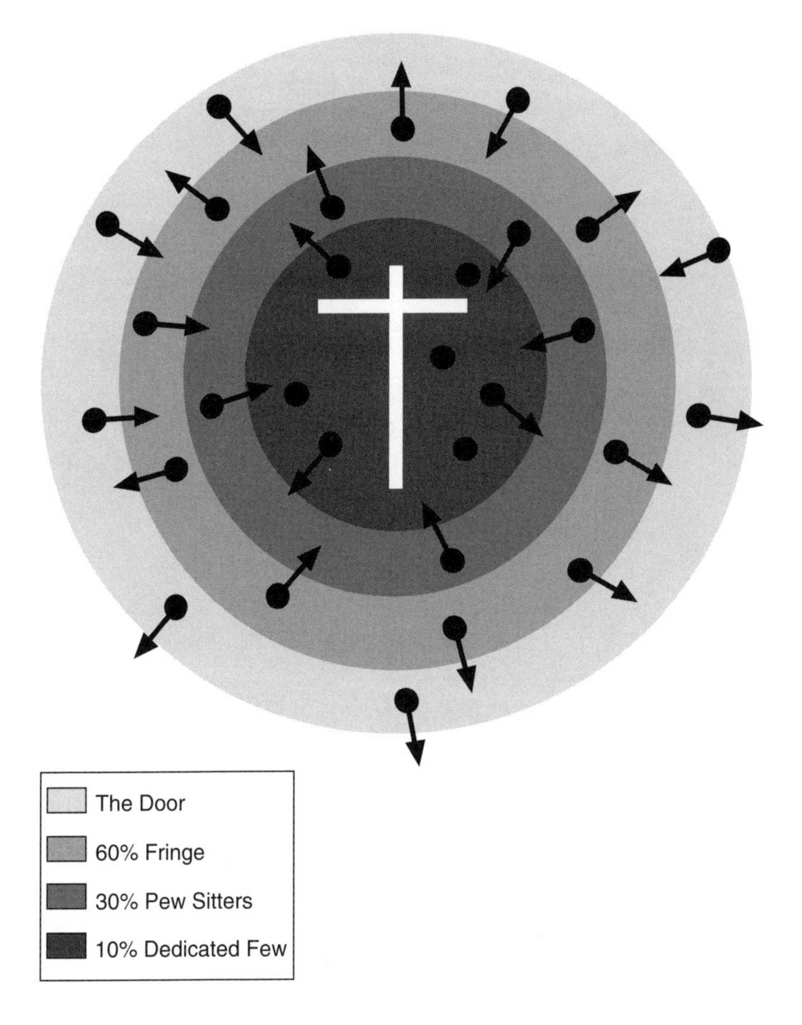

Figure C
Map of Groups in the Church

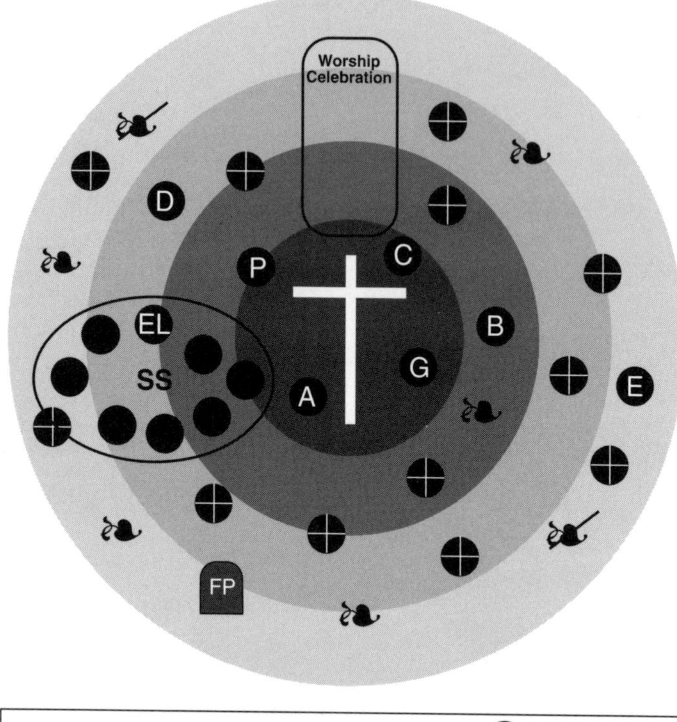

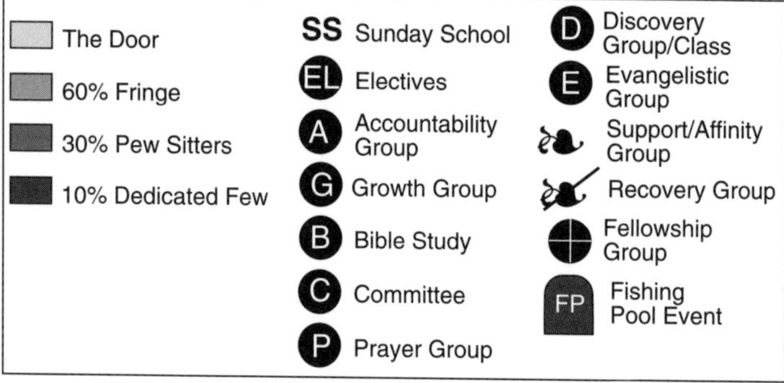

Figure D
Map of Groups in the Church

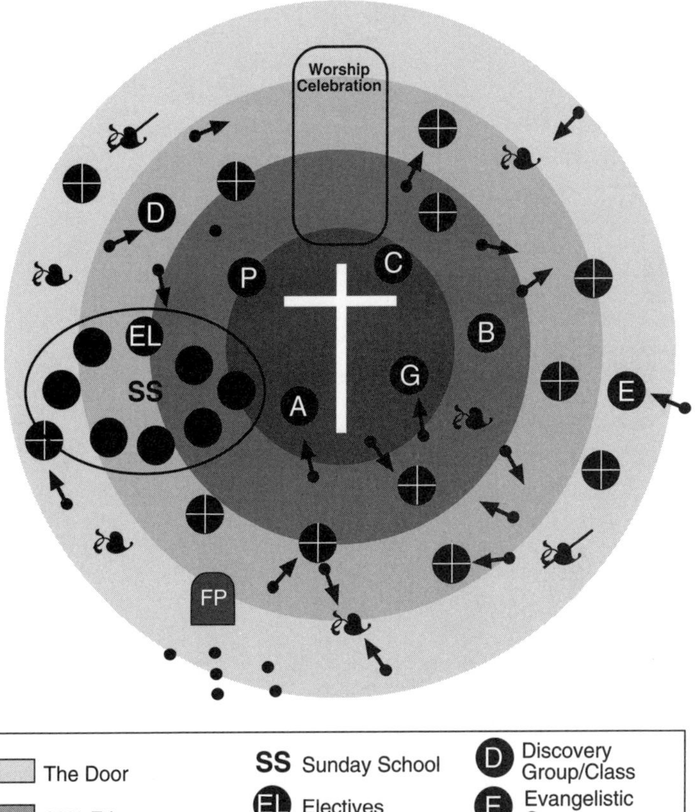

Figure E
Synergy System

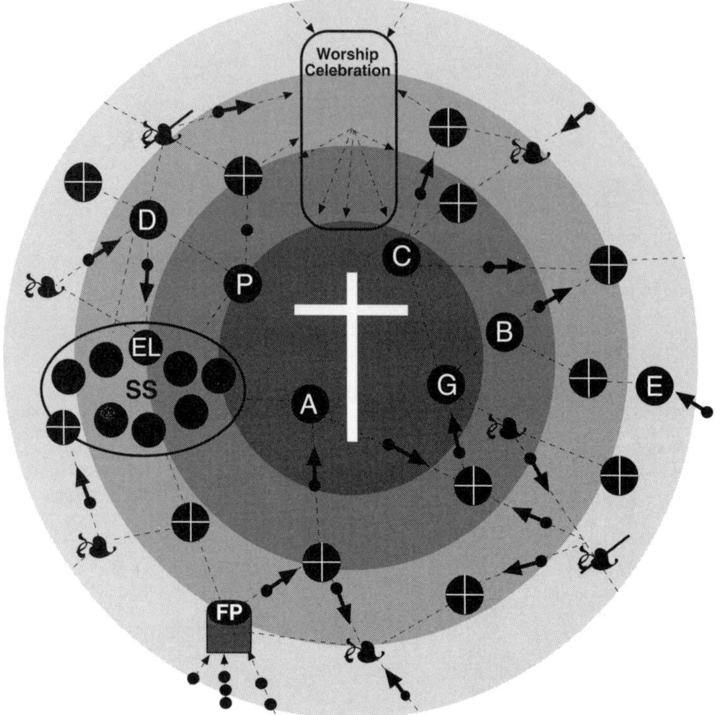

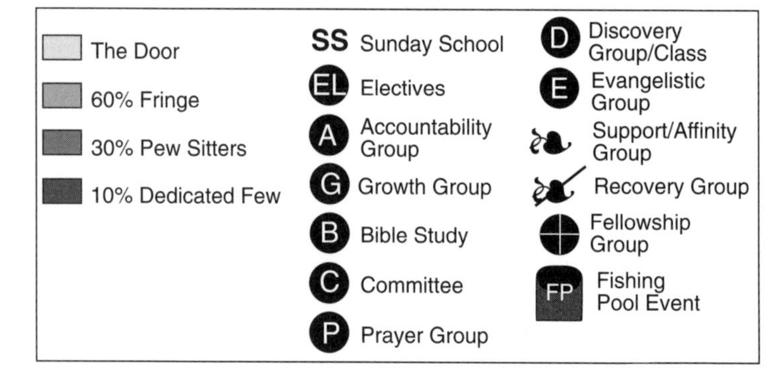

10

How Each Group Works with the Whole Body

Traders Point Christian Church in Indianapolis, Indiana, is an example of a congregation with an integrated system of groups. TPCC considers its adult Bible school classes small groups that meet on Sunday mornings at the church building. The primary focus of these classes is to develop the biblical literacy of class members through Bible study and application. The development of members is also emphasized. Most of these classes have also divided into care groups, Bible studies, and other groups that meet throughout the week in members' homes.

Other small groups include nurture groups, specialized groups (men's and women's groups, a singles' ministry, and a seniors' ministry), support groups, and ministry teams. The graph below shows how each of TPCC's various groups focuses on four different functions. Notice that each type of ministry has some focus on each of the four functions but all to different degrees. TPCC is a good model for a church with integrated groups. The church manages its group life well and is able to disciple people through these various types of groups.

In the following sections each ministry on the Synergy System map presented in chapter 9 is identified, defined, and discussed in terms of where it fits in the integrated system. A chart illustrating how much each group focuses on the four functions is presented for

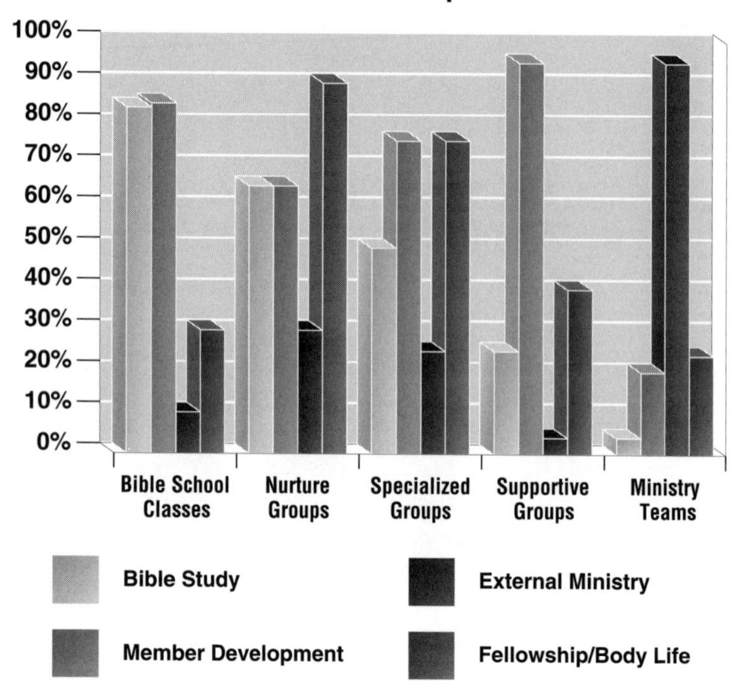

each ministry. These percentages, of course, are general—the focus will be somewhat different even in the same types of groups, and it will change as a group goes through the various stages of its life cycle.

Fellowship Groups

These groups go by a variety of names: fellowship groups, Bible study groups, *koinonia* groups, covenant groups, care groups, sharing groups, cells, kinship circles, or often just small groups. They are the most basic type of group in the system and probably the type most churches would begin with.

These small groups act as connectors or bridges (switching stations) between other groups in the model. Often a person coming out of a support or recovery group, for instance, begins participating in a fellowship group where his or her needs for fellowship, support, care, love, and some accountability are met. Later that person may seek more accountability and disciplined growth with the goal of eventually becoming a leader in the church, so he will move on to a growth group.

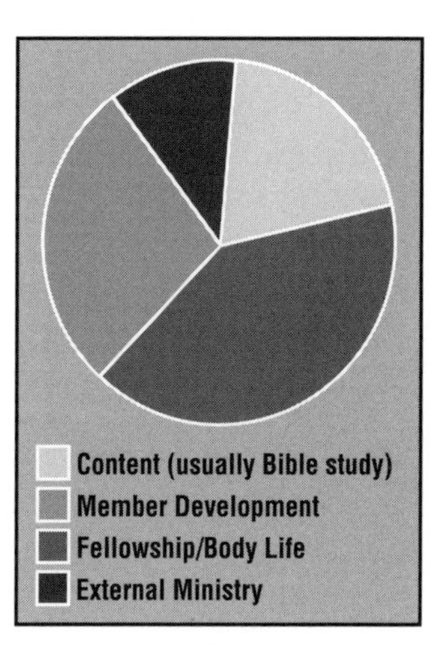

Or a new Christian may graduate from a new-members' class. She needs continued guidance and support in her new life, so she begins participating in a fellowship group. In time that group births a new group, and she becomes an apprentice in that group. Eventually, that group births another new group, and she begins leading a group. Perhaps that group will have a special emphasis, such as a beginners' Bible study (since she is a new Christian), a moms' group (since she has young children), or a prayer group (because she wants to place a special emphasis on prayer in the group).

Fellowship groups are located all over the map. That is because this type of group is flexible. Fellowship groups can act almost like growth groups when the members all want high accountability, are willing to do outside work, and want to grow in Christlikeness and service. This group would not take the place of the growth group but may be situated on the map closer to the center. On the other hand, a fellowship group may be out on the fringe of the church or at the door. This group may emphasize inviting non-Christians to the group. Bible study is entry level, and the atmosphere is relaxed, with no outside work required, low accountability, and a low commitment level. Fellowship groups are located everywhere between these two extremes to meet different types of people where they are. Leaders of these groups have a variety of spiritual gifts and interests, so there is no reason for all of these groups to be exactly the same. Each group should minister where it is, with the combination of gifts and resources available at its disposal.

One warning: These groups should *not* become recovery groups. As will be seen, recovery groups are specialized and often deal with complex and difficult issues. It would be easy for some fellowship groups to slip into pseudorecovery groups if the leaders are not careful. Without adequate training and resources, this could be dangerous.

This is another reason for an integrated system of groups. When a member is pouring out problems the group cannot handle—and oftentimes these problems are draining the group members and not allowing progress in the rest of the group—that member should be tactfully shepherded into an appropriate recovery group or, in some cases, to a trained counselor. A leader can sometimes identify a person with deeper problems than the group can handle by recognizing certain behaviors: monopolizing conversations, constantly taking discussions off track, acting "super spiritual," sharing a plethora of personal problems or playing one-upmanship at prayer request time, or acting in other inappropriate ways during a meeting. Dealing with such a person takes sensitivity, love, compassion, and help from a coach or small group coordinator. How to deal with a person with such problems should be discussed in leaders' meetings. (One good resource for how to deal with difficult individuals or situations is *Small Group Bible Studies: How to Lead Them* by Pat Sikora, Standard Publishing. This same information is also available on the Internet World Wide Web site, The Small Group Network: http://smallgroups.com.)

Bible Study Groups/Specialized Groups

Bible study groups have many of the same characteristics as fellowship groups except for a few key differences: (1) they emphasize content more; (2) they are often—but not always—men's and women's groups; (3) the size of the groups can vary—they can be large, and if so, they are often broken down into smaller groups; and (4) they are usually short term—three months to nine months, for instance. Like fellowship groups, Bible study groups can be good opportunities for outreach—if designed to do so. Men's groups and women's groups particularly can attract the unchurched when they are invited by neighbors, friends, coworkers, or relatives.

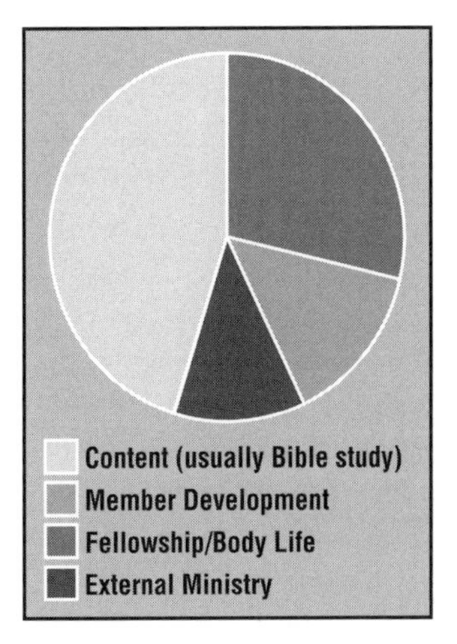

The church should not stop once it has fellowship and Bible study groups started and they are multiplying. Other groups will provide more entry points into the church and more opportunities for people's needs to be met. One group that is essential to continually starting new groups is the growth group.

Growth Groups

Growth groups are located at the center of the map because the middle of the centered set is Jesus. Growth groups help the believer move closer to Christ and live like and for him. In response to this growth, the Christian takes on a ministry according to his spiritual gifts, the leading of the Holy Spirit, and the needs of the church and community.

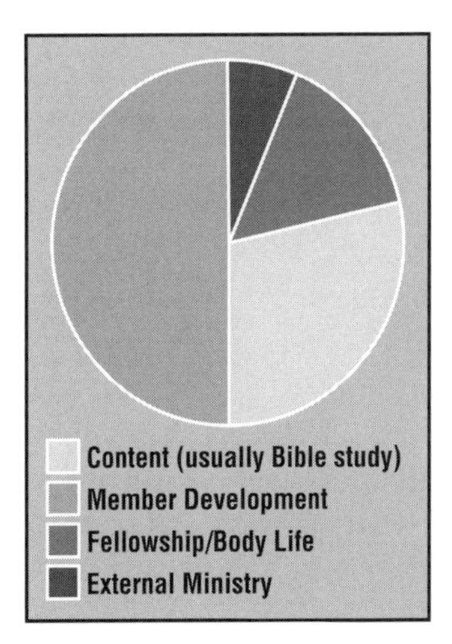

Growth groups go by several names: usually discipleship or accountability groups (not to be confused with four- or five-member accountability groups). The Navigators discipleship groups are called "2:7 groups" (from Col. 2:7). Churches Alive also specializes in growth groups.

Christians at different levels of spiritual maturity grow in their relationship with Christ through these groups. They usually meet two hours a week either at the church building or in a member's home. Participants come prepared for each meeting by having completed one to two hours of homework, including Bible study and Scripture memorization. Usually a group is comprised of no more than fourteen members. Depending on the curriculum, participants usually commit to eighteen to twenty-four months. However, some church leaders have found this to be too long—people sometimes burn out after about a year. But growth requires time—maturity in Christ cannot be rushed. Four emphases are usually included: Bible discussion (about 50 percent), sharing (about 15 percent), prayer (about 15 percent), and outreach training (about 20 percent).

The growth group is the training ground for leaders of new-members' classes, Sunday school classes, youth ministries, and small groups, as well as for deacons, elders, and other leaders in the church. A scriptural basis for growth groups comes from 1 Timothy 2:2 and Hebrews 5:2. These verses indicate that a purpose of Christian education is to produce teachers of others.

Growth groups may not be for everyone. This is the place for the dedicated 10 percent on Coleman's target (although the goal is to eventually include much more than 10 percent of the congregation). Some folks may feel their spiritual maturity needs are being met in worship services, Sunday school, or fellowship groups. The goals of these groups may include developing a hunger for spiritual growth in those people and ultimately shepherding some of them into a growth group.

The growth group is fundamental in the Synergy System. Members are the future leaders of other groups in the church. The more people in the congregation go through growth groups, the more the church can expand its ministry and outreach. Once new leaders are produced through growth groups, other ministries can be added. One group that is similar to the growth group is the accountability group.

Accountability Groups

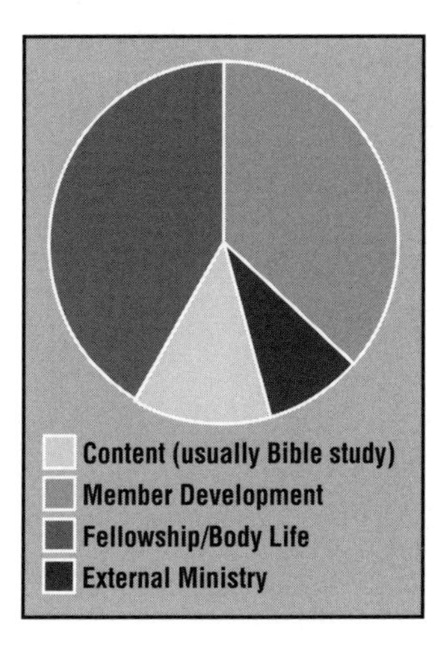

Accountability groups usually consist of two to four people of the same sex. These groups meet for about an hour, at a time that is convenient for all participants. At each meeting, members ask one another questions about their spiritual life or ministry, they encourage one another, and they pray with and for each other. Accountability questions and spiritual goals are set up by the members. Accountability questions may include questions like: How have you shared your faith since we last met? What steps have you taken to accomplish your spiritual goals? Did you take time out to pray each day this week? Have you just told me a lie?

In these groups, members strive to reach the point where they can remove the mask so often worn in Christian circles. With authenticity as a prerequisite of accountability, each member must be willing to expose vulnerable areas. Confidentiality, mutual encouragement, and common spiritual goals make being transparent easier. Deeper friendships with other members and with God often result.

On the map, accountability groups are close to the center. Sharing personal concerns often occurs in accountability groups because the participants are of the same sex and the group is small. Because of the highly personal level of sharing and confession, confidentiality is essential in the accountability group. People who are already leaders in the church are the most likely participants in these groups, although certainly not exclusively so.

Support Groups

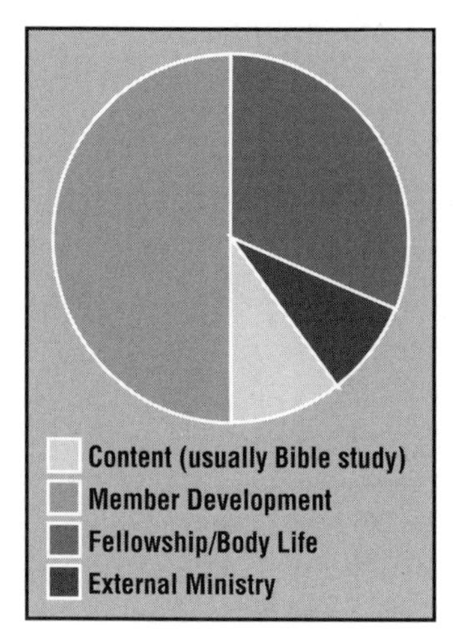

In support groups, members share a common interest or need. These groups are less intense than recovery groups in that mutual support, not healing, is the primary objective of the group's existence. Support groups may also be called affinity groups. They include groups for single mothers, writers, people with aging parents, people with the same hobbies, people with physical disabilities, and so forth. The kinds of support groups are almost innumerable.

Support groups are positioned on the map between the fringe and the door because these groups are good opportunities for outreach. Unchurched individuals who would not attend a Bible study group or Sunday school class will often participate in a group that meets their felt needs. So support groups provide entry points to the congregation.

They also are helpful for church members. Often in a person's cycle of spiritual growth it is beneficial to be with others who share the same needs or concerns. A diabetic may learn better care for his health in such a group and get emotional support and encouragement. At the same time, he will receive spiritual guidance and support, as other like-minded people pray for and with him, share how the Lord has helped them cope, and study the Scriptures together to find what God's Word says to them in their particular situation.

Support groups interact with other groups in many ways. Sometimes a support group is started out of a Sunday school class. For instance, several people in a class discover they all have parents with cancer. So they begin a support group among themselves. One of the participants has a friend at work who is in the same situation, so she invites the coworker. Others invite brothers or sisters, neighbors, and acquaintances to the group. Thus the group is not only a support to the initial members, but an outreach as well.

Those who come into the church through support groups should eventually be shepherded into Sunday school classes, new-members' classes, fellowship groups, or other groups. Support groups do not go on forever. They can easily become closed and internalized without guidance. The empty chair can be used in support groups to keep them open if that is desired. If the group decides meetings should be closed after several weeks, then the group should not last more than about two years. At that time participants can break out to birth new support groups or become involved in other groups, such as a growth group.

Recovery Groups

A recovery group meets to help members deal with and recover from certain problems. Recovery groups include those that deal with addictions, divorce, the death of a spouse or other family member, codependency, overeating, and other problems. Some recovery groups follow a Twelve-Step format in a Christian manner. Members of recovery groups share a common need and help support one another as they seek healing to become whole persons in Christ.

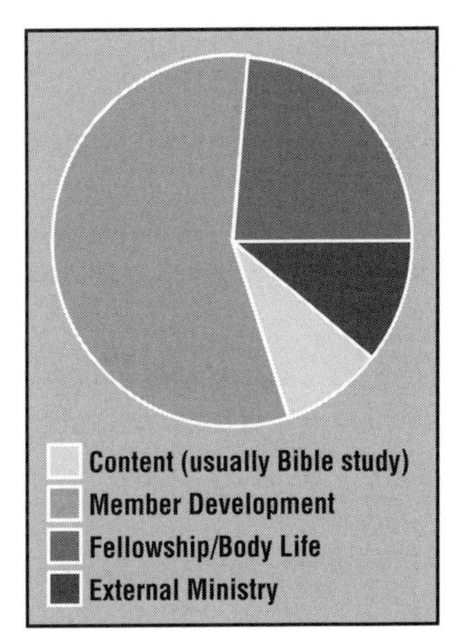

Recovery groups, like support groups, are entry points into the congregation. They are an excellent opportunity to reach people who are hurting or trying to get through some difficulty in their lives. Recovery groups should be led either by someone who has previously gone through a similar group or someone who is well trained to lead such a group.

Recovery groups are much more than outreach opportunities, however. Many people in churches are hurting, dependent, addicted, abused, neglected, ashamed, or involved in some sinful lifestyle. Before church members can be salt and light to a needy world, they may need healing and recovery themselves. Often people in Sunday school classes or fellowship groups display behaviors that indicate they may need to be in some type of recovery group. Leaders should be sensitive to those behaviors and help shepherd those people into groups where they can get help.

On the other hand, individuals eventually "graduate" from recovery groups. How will the church continue to help them? They need continued support, encouragement, love, and care, although hopefully to a lesser degree. Leaders in the church should shepherd them into fellowship groups, accountability groups, or growth groups that can give them the support they need. Accountability or growth groups may work well if the person continues to seek the high accountability received in the recovery group.

Adult Sunday School Classes

The adult Sunday school has been discussed in detail throughout the book, particularly in chapters 5–8. Here I will show how it fits in the Synergy System.

Adult Sunday school is one of the most difficult ministries to place in the system. While it is generally homogeneous, the Sunday school is more heterogeneous than many of the groups. At least in design, the Sunday school includes people in all dif-

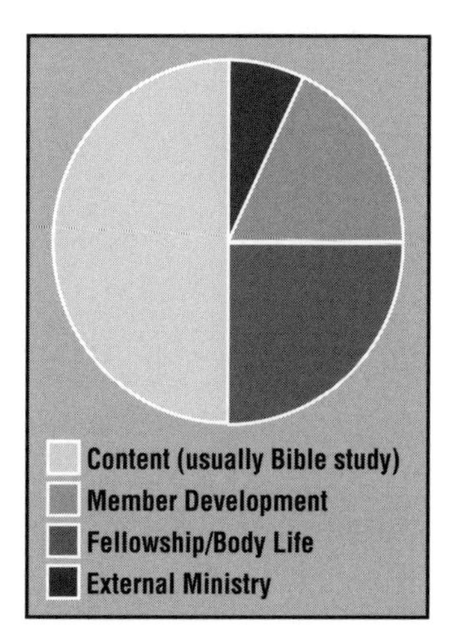

ferent stages of their spiritual development. So it is located on the map about midway in the audience target. But it is intended to reach both the people at the door and the committed 10 percent of the congregation—and everyone in between.

Notice on the map that one fellowship group actually appears to be a part or an appendage of the Sunday school. Some large adult classes can begin their own small groups that meet during the week in members' homes. These groups may consist solely of members, or include people not in any other group in the church and unchurched friends and neighbors. Such a group may be an outreach not just for the church, but for that particular Sunday school class as well. This is one good way of beginning the integration process in a church that has a traditional adult Sunday school program and wants to start small groups.

The topics or method of Bible study in ongoing Sunday school classes should be open, so that Christians and non-Christians alike can feel welcome and be able to apply the lessons. But Christians who are growing in maturity and service need to study deeper subjects, and they need to be equipped for service. Where will this happen if not in the Sunday school class?

Elective Classes

One place is in short-term elective classes. These classes can focus on a particular area of concern, such as witnessing, and be, in effect, closed to anyone not part of the select group of people they are designed for. In such classes, equipping members for service and in certain areas of knowledge contributes toward the goal of making disciples.

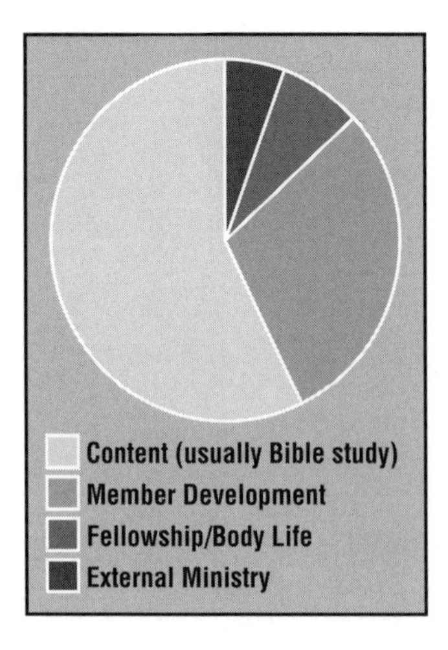

Electives and the ongoing adult Sunday school work hand in hand in the Synergy System. They can be viewed as a two-track Sunday school, providing need-oriented elective classes as well as systematic Bible studies for people in specific age groups and life stages. The number of ongoing classes and the number of elective classes depends on several variables: the average age of the congregation (more older members would likely stay in ongoing fellowships), the needs of the church and the community, the percentage of the congregation that expresses a desire for particular elective classes, the overall preference of the congregation, the size of the congregation, and other factors. Members could continue to be in their ongoing fellowship groups, where they receive support, encouragement, and the sense of community they need, but attend elective classes of interest from time to time. In a healthy Sunday school atmosphere, the members of the ongoing class should be supportive of members' desires to become better equipped in specific areas and to grow in service.

Elective classes can be on a variety of subjects, as many as there are needs in the church, including teacher training, counseling, witnessing (lifestyle evangelism), family concerns, single parenting, music, preaching, gift analysis, church planting, and missionary training. Special classes can also be offered on particular books of the Bible, prophecy, apologetics, Greek, Hebrew, church history, and so forth for church members. Growth groups can also be included in elective classes on Sunday mornings.

Some Sunday school electives can be targeted specifically for the door of the church. One such class is a "honeymooners' class." This is a class specifically for newlyweds, and it takes a topical approach to study. Church members can let friends and family members who are newly married know about this class. And people getting married at the church building can be strongly encouraged to take the class. This is just one example of a door class.

Even some support groups can be offered as part of the elective program—even on Sunday morning. Short-term groups for people who are deaf, divorced, single parents, or caregivers of sick or elderly parents, for instance, could be offered.

Courses can include field trips, on-site training (such as visiting a prison in a prison ministry class), viewing videos (for example, watching a James Dobson film in a parenting class), or other activities. There is no sacred time frame for electives. Sunday mornings and evenings and Saturday mornings are popular, but any time that people can meet is acceptable.

Small churches might offer one class a quarter; larger churches can offer a wide variety of classes. In fact, this is an area in which churches can cooperate with one another. For instance, a church with a large building can invite several smaller churches to be a part of their elective classes. Perhaps the smaller churches have teachers with specific areas of expertise who can teach some of the classes. Working together in this way can help bring unity where there has been competition in the past.

One important caution for establishing elective classes: They should be brought in slowly and with good communication. If people think the "traditional" Sunday school program is being overrun by electives and that the leadership pool is being drained, irreversible problems can arise. Introducing elective classes should be done with as much thought, planning, and care as beginning small groups, which has been discussed earlier.

Two other classes—the new-members' class and the discovery class—are part of the Sunday school and have their own distinct purposes.

New-Members' and Discovery Classes

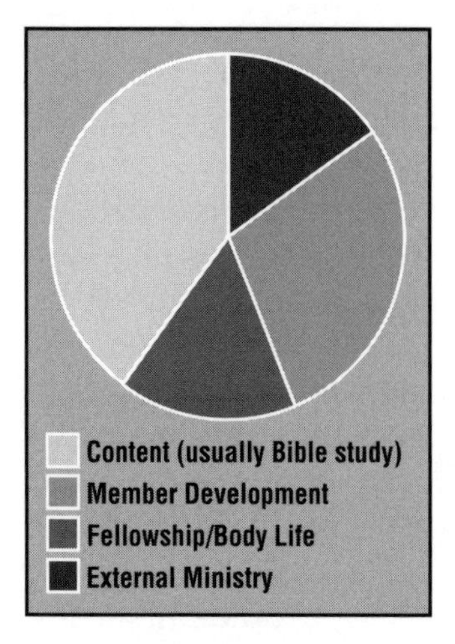

New-members' classes and discovery classes are located in the fringe of the church but are available to people at the door. These classes are both an evangelistic and an assimilation tool.

In general, the new-members' class orients people to the church and the opportunities available for growth and service. It is open, as the name indicates, to new members of the church, but it is usually also open to others seeking more information about the church. These people could be potential transfers or unbelievers. Normally, members of this class have an understanding of the gospel but are seeking information about the church.

The discovery class, on the other hand, grounds people in the Christian faith and the beginning of their walk with Christ. It is a "Christianity 101" class, and its attenders could range from seekers to new members to people who are newly awakened in their faith, whether new Christians or long-time believers. Even those who have been church members for a long time may be interested in the discovery class or group. Many people in the church do not feel they really know the basics of the gospel—especially well enough to share their faith with others. The discovery class helps get people started on the path to discipleship. It is a precursor to the growth group or accountability group. The basics of Christianity—assurance of salvation, answered prayer, victory over temptation, guidance, and God's forgiveness—are the truths studied in Churches Alive's discovery classes. It is important to help new members become familiar with their Bibles and how to study the Scriptures, as well as with some important doctrines of the Christian faith.

Often discovery classes meet on Sunday mornings. Proximity to worship and the availability of free child care make this an excellent time. Discovery groups can meet at the church building or in people's homes on weekday evenings as well.

At some time during discovery classes or new-members' classes, participants are introduced to continuing opportunities for spiritual growth through growth groups, fellowship groups, adult Sunday school, and so forth. Leaders try to involve participants in the life of the church, thereby assimilating them into the body. Leaders of these groups can be growth group graduates, elders, deacons, or staff members.

Evangelistic Bible Studies

These groups are also called "investigative Bible studies" or "beginners' Bible studies." Christians can invite non-Christian friends to investigate the Bible with them—to investigate who Jesus is and the claims he made about himself. Here are seven steps for beginning an evangelistic Bible study for friends and neighbors.

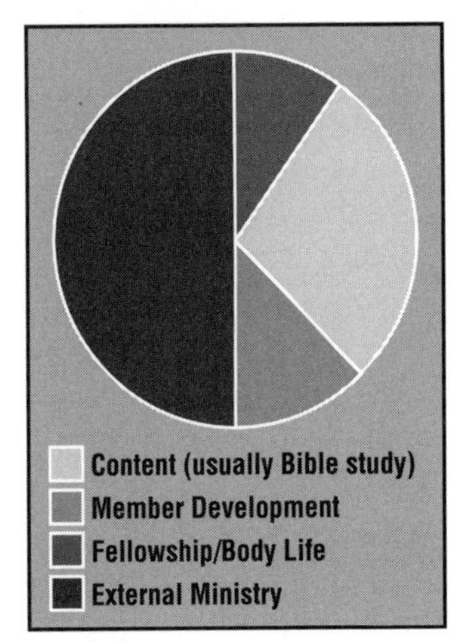

1. Set a time and place for the meeting. Keep it short, usually no longer than one hour.
2. Choose a time that is relatively free from conflicts.
3. Set a definite duration, such as ten weeks. People will not respond to something that seems to last forever.
4. Meet in someone's home or apartment, which has

plenty of room, is comfortable (air-conditioned in summer), and is convenient for participants to get to.
5. Visit friends and neighbors. Get to know them better and look for opportunities to bridge from small talk to personal conversation to mild discussions about faith. When appropriate, invite them to investigate the Bible *with* you.
6. Ask them if they would like to invite other friends or neighbors to the group. Make this an opportunity for a budding community to develop.
7. Begin and end meetings on time.

Investigative Bible studies work particularly well in apartment buildings. There are many opportunities to befriend neighbors—in the hallway, elevator, laundry room, swimming pool—and eventually invite them to investigate the Bible. A sense of community can be fostered easily in an apartment complex when Christians initiate real friendships, not just relationships for the sake of evangelizing the building.

Heidi and I wanted to start an investigative Bible study in our forty-unit apartment building a little after we had moved in. But Glen, a staff minister at our church, advised us to wait a while, build relationships with our neighbors, and pray for them. When I asked him how long we should wait before starting the study, he simply said that the Holy Spirit would somehow let us know when the time was right.

"But how will we know when the time is right?" I asked.

"I don't know. But the Holy Spirit will let you know."

That wasn't exactly the answer I was looking for. My pragmatic nature wanted a specific date and a ten-point list of how-to's. But we did what Glen suggested—we waited, made friends, and prayed.

Then one evening about a year and a half later, I was stopped by our apartment manager, Sherry. She told me about Sigma, who had been approached by a member of a church many consider a cult. They had asked Sigma to attend their Bible study. Sherry led me to the pool, where she, Sigma, and three other friends started asking me about this church. None of my friends were Christians, but they knew that I was, and that I might know something about the cult. In the midst of our conversation one of my neighbors, a long-haired young guy who wore black heavy-metal T-shirts and had a reputation for smoking pot, said, "Why don't we start our own Bible study here? Mike could lead it and we could meet at different people's apartments each week. We could invite other people from the building too!"

The building of relationships and dependence on the Holy Spirit are indispensable in starting evangelistic studies. It is true that people don't care how much you know until they know how much you care. Those budding relationships and the work of the Spirit are equally important as you continue leading the group week by week and as you seek to lead them to accept Christ as their Lord and Savior. The relationships we built and the Bible study we eventually led planted many seeds.

What happened with that evangelistic study? Vic, Sigma's boyfriend, was the first one in our group to name Christ as his Savior. I baptized him early one chilly Sunday morning in the apartment swimming pool. People from the building stood at their windows and watched him being immersed. It took Sigma more than a year before she made the same decision.

Now both are part of our ongoing fellowship group. They are growing in their relationships with the Lord and with fellow Christians. Slowly but surely they are being transformed into the image of Christ. Now they are sharing their faith with their neighbors, people they work with, and even complete strangers! And they are beginning to get involved in the ministry of the church. They are being nurtured through their fellowship group and Sunday school class—their inward journeys toward the center of the Synergy System—and challenged to begin focusing on others in ministry. They are being transformed into the image of Christ as his disciples.

For more help starting and running investigative Bible studies, read *Introducing Jesus* by Peter Scazzero (InterVarsity

Press). It gives not only lots of practical tips for starting such groups but also six studies that can be used with non-Christians to bring them face-to-face with Jesus.

Committees, Leadership Teams, and Ministry Teams

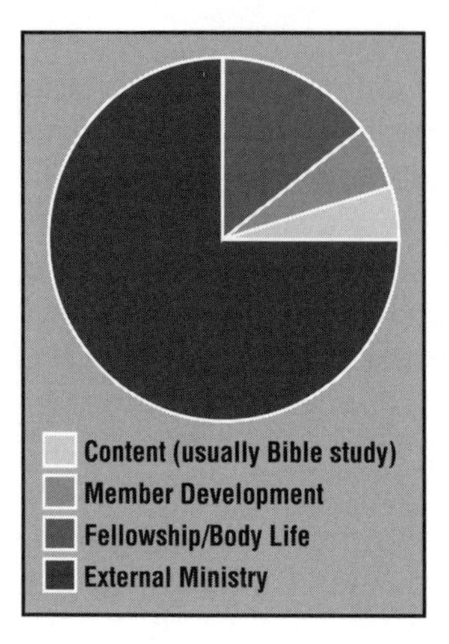

Roberta Hestenes writes much about turning committees into communities. Committees can be communities when members pray for and with each other and care for one another.

Committees, leadership teams (elders, deacons, and so forth), and ministry teams are placed close to the middle of the map because the dedicated few are members of such groups. Some of the members have graduated from a growth group and may continue in an accountability group. These groups may "run" the organization of the church, but they need nurture, care, and opportunities for spiritual growth as well. So they act much like a fellowship group that has a specific mission. For more information about these groups, see Hestenes's book *Turning Committees into Communities.*

Celebration Events

Celebration is part of Peter Wagner's formula for the healthy church: celebration + congregation + cell = church. Large-group events help bring a sense of unity, fellowship, and cohesion among church members, especially in a large church. And of course, the pulpit cannot be ignored as both an avenue for

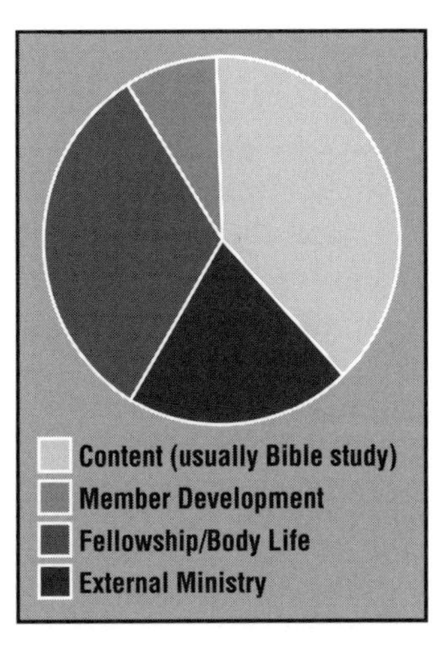

Christian education and Bible learning and an opportunity to reach non-Christians. As the chart shows, content is the predominate focus. Content in this case is preaching and worship (although worship also has fellowship and member-development qualities).

The celebration event fits into the overall ministry of the church of groups by being a place where visitors and members hear about the different opportunities for growth available in the church. This can be accomplished by promoting small groups as a part of services, in church programs, and on display tables before and after services.

Community Christian does an excellent job of promoting their small groups. Preaching Minister Dave Ferguson speaks about the values of being in a small group in a natural way during his message in their seeker-oriented service. Groups are mentioned during announcements in the service. The weekly program handed out on Sunday mornings includes several messages about groups. On the inside cover each week is this statement:

> Small Groups—A Place for You
>
> Are you looking for a place to meet some new friends? Does exploring the truths of the Bible interest you? Would you like to find out how others are growing in their relationship with God? If so, then a small group is for you! For more information, take a few minutes to stop by the small group display in the reception area or look over the insert in your program.

A table is set up every Sunday in the reception area with information about groups. Additionally, leaders and apprentice leaders are active during seeker services, getting to know visitors and looking for opportunities to invite them to their small groups.

By keeping small groups in front of people on a regular basis, the church demonstrates that groups are important and that being in a group is a normal part of being involved in the church.

Small group leaders at Community Christian also attend other events—seminars and workshops on subjects such as divorce recovery—and invite people to their groups. At some of these events people are invited to special support groups that are on the same subject as the seminar. Events such as these are commonly called "fishing pool" events.

Fishing Pools

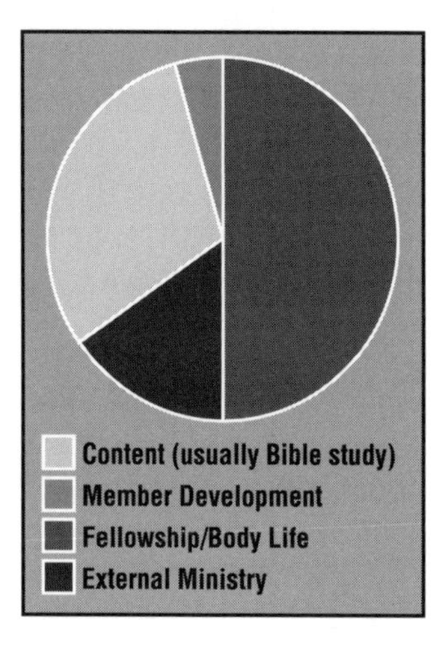

Many church buildings are designed with large halls or auditoriums, or both. Americans today enjoy unique and special experiences, especially when they are shared with other people. Many people go to bars to watch sporting events together. The same kind of gathering—minus the alcohol, of course—can be held at church buildings. George Barna speaks about "value-added marketing." He says that churches can use their buildings to host debates, show major sporting events, and conduct other events, and then add to that program a special speaker, giveaways, or some other "bonus" that will encourage people to attend.[1]

Many people who normally might not go into a church building will come, experience the community, and discover they can actually have fun in "church." They can learn that the church does meet real needs and is relevant. These kinds of events make the church part of the community, as it should be—part of the social glue that holds the community together. Announcements can be made at these events promoting upcoming events: support or recovery groups, open retreats, open gym nights, and so forth.

The types of events are as various as the imagination of church leaders: seminars on family, abuse, AIDS, finances, single parenting, and other topics; banquets with local Christian celebrities as speakers; showing of the baseball All-Star game, the Super Bowl, and other major sporting events on a large-screen TV—adding snacks, a soft drink bar, and local Christian sports celebrities to speak after the game or at half-time. Leaders of various groups can utilize these events to meet people and invite them to share in their group with them. This is where the "fishing" comes in.

All of the various ministries and small groups listed above are integrated on the map to help the church not just make converts, but make disciples by providing an array of opportunities for spiritual growth. But the model is not complete without one essential aspect: leadership. Even in a well-integrated system, the people need to be shepherded into groups where they can continue their process of growth.

Leadership

Who is going to oversee the group life of the church? Should this be one person, or should there be a leader over each area: adult Sunday school, small fellowship groups, support and recovery groups, and so forth? What should the leadership structure look like in an integrated church? These questions cannot be answered here. Many leadership books and conferences are available to help churches make these decisions. Carl George deals with many of these issues in *Prepare Your Church for the Future;* Larry Richards deals with some of them in *A New Face for the Church*, particularly chapter 16; and several other authors also consider these issues in their books. Dale Galloway has written several books in conjunction with 20/20 Vision, the cell group ministry of New Hope Community Church in Portland, Oregon, which he pastors. These books, along with his seminars, provide many good tips on building and leading a cell group church.

Leadership is an essential consideration if group life is to be "managed" well, if programs are to be coordinated so they work well with one another, and if people are to be shepherded or directed to the appropriate groups for their spiritual growth. Who this person—or people—is depends on the circumstances of the congregation. In a small church, for example, it might be the senior minister or perhaps a volunteer Christian education minister. Whoever this person is, he or she is responsible for overseeing the entire body life of the church. At least one person in every congregation should know what is going on in all the programs and groups of the church so that an uninterrupted flow of ministry can continue.

The senior minister is extremely important in the group life of the church, especially as small groups are being implemented. Lyman Coleman says, "Effective small group ministries flourish when the Senior Pastor places a high priority on groups and cheerleads from the pulpit every Sunday."[2] David Yonggi Cho also says the pastor must be the key person involved in the formation of groups. He speaks of one large church in the United States that wanted to start small groups. The pastor visited Seoul and saw the value of cells. But instead of being the key person involved in starting the groups, he turned all the responsibilities over to an associate pastor. After two years the program was stagnant. Attendance was poor and members were not motivated toward evangelism. Why? Cho answers:

> The congregation sees cell groups as only one of many varied programs in this big church. They don't see them as the key to

> revival or to evangelism; after all, there are so many other programs aimed at those goals. The pastor isn't actively involved, so the members feel that cell groups can't be all that important.
>
> If cell groups are to succeed, the pastor must become so convinced of their necessity in the church that he will see them as the key to the life or death of his church. Once he becomes convinced, the program will move.[3]

Cho believes the senior pastor must commit his time and energy to laying the groundwork for the ministry. After the program is going, he should remain the obvious leader, training and motivating leaders. He can delegate details to an associate minister or some other person, but the real leadership remains with the pastor, he says.

Lyle Schaller uses a list of critical questions to help churches appraise their group life. These questions should be asked of leaders who want to implement the integrated system of groups proposed in this chapter.[4]

1. Who is responsible for the general oversight, care, and nurture of the group life of your congregation?
2. Who is responsible for counseling groups in need of revitalization?
3. Who is responsible for maintaining the health of existing groups?
4. Who will take the initiative to organize new groups in response to the changing needs of people?
5. Who makes sure that loyal leaders and workers are recognized and thanked?
6. Who will help newcomers find a home in one of the groups in your congregation?
7. Who will repeatedly affirm the value and importance of each group to the members of that group as well as to others?
8. Who will help each group see the need for an occasional "regluing" of group ties?
9. Who is responsible for the group life in your congregation?

One important principle for leadership in all groups is this: Before adding additional groups, departments, and programs, the healthy church expands its base of leadership. When leaders are weighed down by more and more responsibilities, burnout is the result. Before beginning a ministry of small groups, the church needs to have leaders in place instead of adding "small group leader" to the job description of already overburdened leaders.

The leadership base can be expanded by starting small "turbo" groups of potential leaders with the expectation that everyone in those initial groups will eventually lead groups of their own. Another way to expand the leadership base is by having apprentice leaders in all groups, especially fellowship groups. With that procedure a corps of leaders who will birth new groups in the future is always in training. Growth groups are another way of expanding the leadership base. "Graduates" become leaders of new groups.

Leadership training is essential to the success and effectiveness of all groups in the church. A plethora of leadership training resources is available to churches. (If you are on the Internet, check out The Small Group Network on the World Wide Web: http://smallgroups.com.) The thriving and productive churches of small groups are those that have regular leadership meetings along with occasional specialized opportunities for training, such as seminars, workshops, conferences, and retreats.

Another principle is that leaders must also have growth opportunities. Many times in a church the only groups that leaders are involved in are those they lead. They should try to be involved in at least one group a year in which they are not leading all the time. That might be in their ongoing Sunday school class, where they receive support, encouragement, prayer, and the fellowship they need to be whole people in Christ. Leaders are disciples too, and they need to continue learning, developing, and growing in their Christian lives.

Of the five reasons that many American small group ministries fail, as reported in *Ministries Today* (May/June 1993), three have to do with poor leadership:

1. American small group programs lack sufficient ministerial involvement. If staff ministers are not personally involved in the ministry, says David Yonggi Cho, it is doomed to failure.
2. American small group ministries are guided with little or no vision. Cho says churches in the United States stay small because they think small. "The number one requirement for having real church growth—unlimited church growth—is to set goals," says Cho.
3. Leaders are selected and trained haphazardly. Cho's leaders must be willing to "contract" at least ten hours a week for one year. Leadership training is essential to effective, dynamic, growing groups.

All of these reasons can also be cited for the failure—or at least the inability to accomplish what they should be able to achieve—of other church groups and programs, including the adult Sunday school.

Mapping Spiritual Development

A big part of the leader's role in the Synergy System is to help people find the right groups for where they are in their spiritual journeys. This, of course, is not an exact science. To help you think through the process, here is a list of people who might visit or already be in your congregation. How would you shepherd each of these individuals? First, list the group you would want to get him or her into now. Then list the group(s) he might move into next (either inward toward Christlikeness or outward into ministry). Perhaps think of one or two real people for each of these examples. You do not have to limit yourself to these categories—you may think of people you know who do not match any of these.

- an unbeliever with limited or no relationships with church members
- an unbeliever who has several Christian friends
- an unbeliever involved in non-Christian religions or cults
- an unbeliever with emotional or relational problems
- an unbeliever with mental or physical disabilities
- an unbeliever who is opposed to the gospel
- an unbeliever with limited knowledge of the gospel
- an unbeliever with some church background
- a believer with limited church background and marginal faith
- a first-time visitor to church services who is new in town and has no relationships with church members
- a first-time visitor who has come with a friend
- a believer with many friends but not growing in his faith
- a believer with emotional or relational difficulties
- a believer with mental or physical disabilities
- a church member with few close relationships in the church
- a disciple who is looking for opportunities to grow and serve
- a disciple with leadership potential
- a burned-out leader

You can add other traits to this list, such as age, marital status, life circumstances, interests, and a number of other factors that could help determine how to help each of these people find their place in the church. It is the wide variety of possibilities that makes this challenging. But it is the potential that makes it exciting. If leaders can help people grow in their spiritual walks and eventually in serving others, a heavy weight of feeling like we need to do it all will be lifted off of us. As leaders our main responsibility is to equip others to serve, and I believe the Synergy System can help us do that.

In the last three chapters I have suggested many ideas that would mean change in congregations. But *change* can be a dirty word in some churches, and leaders need to know how to implement it.

11

Making the Changes

"We never did it that way before!" Ralph Neighbour describes these words as "the seven last words of the church" (in his book *The Seven Last Words of the Church*). Some individuals, groups, and even entire churches resist change as if they were resisting Satan. Others are so involved in their own goals or programs that they do not see any need for change or for the higher overall commitments of the church. These attitudes are not healthy for groups in the church.

The once-dependable strongholds of family, neighborhood, and job are shaky in today's world. Baby boomers have grown up under conditions not faced by any other generation: high mobility and high stress. They go to church for friendship and fellowship (50 percent), for Bible study (41 percent), and to be encouraged and inspired (37 percent), according to George Barna.[1] To meet the needs of this segment of the population, the church will need to be flexible enough to make the necessary changes.

Baby boomers may enter your church building with a strong dose of cynicism for the church. They lived through the sixties and seventies, a period in which all institutional structures were looked upon with suspicion. They have seen the highly publicized downfall of public religious figures. And chances are they have experienced some type of family dysfunction, or have known someone who did. Chances are also good that they live hundreds or thousands of miles from family. They are looking for friends but want sincerity most of all—from friends as well as from the church as a whole. One of the primary things that turns boomers off is what they perceive as hypocrisy. They have many felt needs, and in many cases, they are looking for help. Whether they realize it or not, they are looking for God. Many are open to the gospel. How will we reach them and keep them?

Leaders must manage well the group life of their churches to meet needs and to help people map out their course of spiritual discovery and growth. Boomers want relational churches, but they also want organized, well-planned, high-quality experiences. The church cannot afford haphazard planning, events and studies that are seemingly unrelated to real life, institutionalized programs that exist for no other reason than tradition, and programs that exist in a ministerial vacuum.

Baby busters—also called Generation X—are much different than their parent boomers. While it is impossible to accurately describe this generation, some generalizations can be helpful in reaching it. (In fact, one generalization is that busters want to be seen as unique individuals, so they really dislike being generalized.) Busters have been described as a generation of busted dreams, busted ambitions, and busted trust. Many are children of divorce. They grew up in isolation with broken promises. They are often cynical because of this and because they have witnessed the fall of public heroes, including high-profile clergy. They may devalue themselves and human life in general because of the rise of abortion, reported child abuse, in-vitro fertilization, genetic testing, and other such developments during their lifetimes. Their parents, the "Me Generation," may have been so self-absorbed that these children received little personal attention. They are the "latchkey kid" generation.

This generation has dealt with tragedy more than their parents. Most teens and young adults have had several friends die—in car accidents, random incidents of violence, drug overdoses, suicides—and so many live life as if they will not live to old age. Boomers smoked pot and most have not had any adverse long-term consequences. Busters snort crack cocaine and die. Boomers brought in a wave of "free sex" and brought on the sexual revolution. Busters have sex with a partner and contract the AIDS virus. Busters are not quick to take on responsibility—adolescence has stretched from a range of age thirteen to seventeen to age eleven to twenty-eight. They enter adolescence younger as they become active in sex earlier, and they remain in it longer, refusing to grow up.

Busters are noncommittal. Their theme is, Leave your options open. Their consumer mind-set—shop around and find the best value, and if you wait long enough the price will come down anyway or the product will be improved, or both—transfers into other areas of life, including their choice of religions and churches. Everything is transitory to them, so they do not ever expect to make a long-term commitment. This is the MTV generation—they are used to getting everything in fifteen-second bits. TV gives them instant, bite-size news stories. Busters are generally unfocused and sometimes just uninterested.

Busters get their views about God and religion and spirituality from TV, movies, music, and music videos. From these sources they form distorted views of the gospel and what it means to be a follower of Christ or any other religious system. They don't trust institutional churches because of the fall of TV preachers and the way the media has generally portrayed Christians. At the same time, busters lean to the conservative when they do come to the church. They do not like the liberal tendencies of many mainline denominations.

One more important fact: Busters love change. They hate traditionalism. In fact, they expect change. An institution that does not embrace change readily will have a difficult time attracting busters.

How will leaders respond to these two groups who represent the present and the future of the church? How do we meet their needs? How do we go about making disciples of these individuals? Will one way do it? Will the same old way work? I don't think so. I think the church needs to try to "become all things to all men so that by all possible means [we] might save some" (1 Cor. 9:22). That doesn't mean we have to become worldly to win the worldly, but it does mean that we understand their needs, their culture, their values—and then we plan with those things in mind.

George Barna states that "churches that cling to centuries-old traditions may have the toughest time in the '90s." He says that young adults "are increasingly impatient with organizations that maintain old traditions for the sake of tradition."[2] The church must face the fact that traditionalism and institutionalism have for years drowned out opportunities to disciple the world for Christ. Congregations must bring about a paradigm change before systems can be put in place, before decisions about Sunday school, small groups, and other ministries can be made, and before the church can truly glorify God. Churches must be careful not to "nullify the word of God for the sake of [their] tradition" (Matt. 15:6).

Fears about Small Groups

There are many reasons why traditionalists and others in the church are afraid to integrate small groups into the structure of the church.

False Doctrine

Some use Acts 20:30 to justify their fears regarding small groups: "Even from your own number men will arise and distort the truth in order to draw away disciples after them." Many leaders have seen or heard of churches that started small groups that "split the church by teaching false doctrines." The groups that caused such problems were usually independent of church authority and structures. In fact, some groups' independence was because the leadership of the church would not sanction people meeting away from the church building. This leads to a second fear.

Untrained Leaders

Some people fear turning over the teaching of God's Word to "untrained" nonprofessionals. Larry Richards points out that

> this whole pattern of thinking is a return to pre-Reformation Catholicism. Luther could contend that the meanest peasant with Scripture was mightier than the greatest Pope without it—but we are unwilling to turn the Word of God over to the best-educated generation of Christians the world has ever produced![3]

Furthermore, says Richards, if leaders do not trust the Holy Spirit to faithfully help small group facilitators to interpret his Word, they deny the Scriptures they claim to be protecting. Until recent years Roman Catholics, for the most part, did not study God's Word without the oversight of a priest. Catholics in ages past were told that a priest was necessary to interpret Scriptures for them and that the Bible was dangerous when studied alone. The Catholics' separation of clergy from laity and their lack of personal dependence on Scripture have been significant differences between their belief systems and those of "Bible believing" Christians. These attitudes have changed drastically in the past ten years. Today, many Catholics are involved in personal and small group Bible study. It seems ironic that as Catholics begin personal and group study of the Bible, "Bible believing" Christians are afraid of allowing laypeople to use the Scriptures in small groups!

Cultish Behavior

The fear that groups might imitate a particular cult relates to the fear of false doctrines. Some people are suspicious of small groups because churches they consider to be cults utilize small groups, especially to evangelize. So they equate all small groups with those cults. Fearing small groups because a particular cult uses them is as unfounded as fearing baptism because Jehovah's Witnesses practice it!

Codependency

Some staff ministers or other leaders may feel wounded or jealous because some of their perceived authority is stripped away when small groups are started. Some up-front leaders do not feel as needed because people are being cared for in their groups, they are learning how to apply biblical principles there, and they are growing in dependence on God, which means less dependence on leaders. (Perhaps churches need to start support groups for codependent pastors!) This is a main reason that all leaders, including staff members and elders, should be involved in the process of starting a small group ministry.

Lack of Confidence in Abilities

Some staff ministers may feel they lack the ability to oversee a small group system. They were not taught how to lead leaders in seminary in many cases. Carl George says most ministers actually do have these skills; they just have to learn to use them.[4]

Groups Seem Unnecessary

"We've survived for seventy years without small groups; we've built a large, strong congregation. Why do we need small groups now?" ask some folks in traditional churches. This is a legitimate question, but it does have an answer. Many ministers have recognized a lack of maturity in their congregations. They see that real *koinonia,* intercessory prayer, and mutual support and caring are missing. These concerns motivate church leaders to seek new ways to bring about spiritual growth and discipleship, and one of the main ways of accomplishing those changes is through small groups.

Another reason some people think small groups are unnecessary is because of generational misunderstandings. People born before 1945 have experienced close extended-family ties that many baby boomers have not. So many middle-aged and older adults do not see the need for the relational ties that small groups provide, and they wonder why anyone else would need such forms.

Worldly Innovations

Some people believe small groups are not the work of God but of the world and Satan. Church groups are equated with the secular therapy groups, encounter groups, and sensitivity-training groups of the 1960s and 1970s. Small house groups are sometimes not understood for what they are—rooted in the New Testament. It is somewhat ironic that some of these same traditionalists consider the Sunday school—a man-made institution—unchangeable and nonnegotiable.

Might Hamper the Sunday School

Some think small groups drain the leadership pool for Sunday school. But as has been demonstrated earlier, small groups, especially when properly implemented, and particularly when apprentice leaders and growth groups are used, *add* to the leadership pool. Small groups can augment the Sunday school—when their ministries are harmonious, they are synergistic.

Liberalism

Conservative churches are orthodox in theology. One good principle is to "speak where the Bible speaks and be silent where the Bible is silent." The Bible is mostly silent about methods. We should be conservative in theology—however you define that. But we can be liberal in methodology. The problem is that many churches defend and uphold not only biblical truth but also our particular subculture. New believers and church members of the 1990s are expected to adopt a particular church style of music, language, forms, and culture, much of which is not relevant to everyday life or to the Scriptures.

How is the church to "disciple all nations"? The apostle Paul said he had "become all things to all men so that by all possible means I might save some" (1 Cor. 9:22). One of those means today may be the adult Sunday school—another might be small groups. But some churches act as if Paul had said, "Become one thing to just a few men so that by your man-made, orthodox, 'correct' means you might protect what you've got." Form must always follow function, and the main function of the church is to make disciples. Churches are free to use whatever forms are available and effective, and which follow from that essential function, as long as they are not prohibited in Scripture.

In some cases a church may find it more effective to abandon or phase out its adult Sunday school. This can be an acceptable solution to carrying out the Great Commission in some areas, although it is not advisable for reasons previously stated. However, it may be God's will in some situations to "[set] aside the first to establish the second" (Heb. 10:9). The Hebrew Christians to whom this epistle was written were apparently upset that the temple and its sacrifices had been all but abolished. These Christians needed to understand that God had done away with the temple and sacrifices because Jesus' sacrifice had been made once and for all. It was sufficient. Today the church needs to be attentive to God's moving through his Spirit. Some believers have made up their minds about which structures are sanctified and which are not, leaving no room for God to move.

Dealing with Appropriate Changes

Small groups are often seen as an element of change. A better way of looking at it is to see small groups as *agents* of change in the congregation. The *real* change that is desired is *spiritual,* not physical or structural. Small groups can help make disciples, build relationships that encourage and support, grow people in maturity and service, and build leadership. Most Christians see these as good things. When leadership emphasizes the spiritual transformation desired and that small groups—along with other current forms available in the church—can help bring that transformation about, difficulties such as those discussed here can be lessened in intensity. When small groups are seen as a context in which change can occur, people can feel involved in the transformation process. They thereby feel they are making a contribution to positive changes in the whole church.

Roberta Hestenes gives a warning to those trying to institute a relational dynamic into a church with an institutional mind-set. She says,

> The major difficulty occurs when a new leader with relational, community-building eyes unwisely develops relational programs and emphases to the neglect of people who are more programmatically or institutionally oriented. Doing this risks ending up with two congregations with contradictory goals.[5]

Communication is essential so that both the adherents of Sunday school and small groups can accept and value each others' ministries. They should see themselves as different members of the one body of Christ. Each can do certain things better than the other, and that is acceptable to both. Both are under the one headship of Christ. Fears, suspicions, jealousies, and other clashes between members of the one body bring pain and a decreased ability to disciple the world for Christ.

In some ways it is natural (from a worldly point of view) for some conflicts and misunderstandings to exist between different ministries of the church. The best response to conflicts, says Lyle Schaller, is to "change the conceptual framework." He says that instead of concentrating on the individual components such as Sunday school or small groups, the church should try to "look at the larger picture in order to determine what can be done to make one ministry strengthen and reinforce the other."[6] Leaders are needed to help the ministries complement rather than conflict with each other. The result is synergism, unity, and the increased ability to make disciples.

Finally, Joe Ellis recommends three mottos for every church.[7]

1. Whatever it takes.
2. Why not?
3. There's a way—let's find it.

Conclusion

> Not everyone who says to me, "Lord, Lord," will enter the kingdom of heaven, but only he who does the will of my Father who is in heaven. Many will say to me on that day, "Lord, Lord, did we not prophesy in your name, and in your name drive out demons and perform many miracles?" Then I will tell them plainly, "I never knew you. Away from me, you evildoers!"
>
> Matthew 7:21–23

Churches are filled with people doing religious things—attending church services, taking the Lord's Supper, going to Sunday school, tithing, supporting missionaries, going on mission trips, and so on. But these things, as good as they are, count for nothing if people do not have a relationship with Jesus—knowing him as Savior and Lord. Maturing Christians are humble and obedient like Jesus, seeking not their own will, but the will of the Father (Mark 14:36; Phil. 2:5–8). These are true disciples.

It is time for Christ's church to take his words seriously—to make disciples who have a relationship with him as Lord and Savior. The church must be about the business of making disciples who are also disciple makers—people who are doing the will of their Father. And it is not God's will for anyone to perish, but for everyone to come to repentance (2 Peter 3:9).

Multiplication is the Master's method of discipling the world. How can churches design their programs to use this method? The Synergy System presents a framework for integrating all the programs and groups of the church to strategically and synergistically make disciples and equip them to bring a world that does not know him into a loving relationship with him.

I hope churches will implement some kind of integrated system to help them make disciples and then map out a plan for their spiritual development toward Christlikeness and ministry. God has chosen the church to carry out his will. "He has committed to us the message of reconciliation. We are therefore Christ's ambassadors, as though God were making his appeal through us" (2 Cor. 5:19–20). All kinds of ministries—including small groups and Sunday school—can provide the means by which the church carries out God's work in the world.

Every church is different and must choose for itself what methods will work best. But ultimately, it is God who will build his church. "Many are the plans in a man's heart, but it is the Lord's purpose that prevails" (Prov. 19:21).

NOTES

Introduction

1. Charles Arn, Donald McGavran, and Win Arn, *Growth: A New Vision for the Sunday School* (1980; reprint, Pasadena, Calif.: Church Growth Press, 1987), 24–25.

2. Gene Getz, *Sharpening the Focus of the Church* (Chicago: Moody Press, 1974), 18.

3. Lyle E. Schaller, *The Seven-Day-a-Week Church* (Nashville: Abingdon Press, 1992), 15.

Chapter 1: What's the Purpose?

1. Joe Ellis, "Current Trends to Consider," *Churches Alive Seminar Notebook* (Cincinnati: Standard Publishing, 1973), E-14.

2. Arn, McGavran, and Arn, *Growth,* 24–25.

Chapter 2: Breaking Down the Walls of Churchianity

1. George Barna, *User Friendly Churches: What Christians Need to Know about the Churches People Love to Go To* (Ventura, Calif.: Regal Books, 1991), 25.

2. Lawrence O. Richards, *A New Face for the Church* (Grand Rapids: Zondervan, 1970), 51.

3. Ellis, "Current Trends to Consider," E-14.

4. Ibid., E-21.

5. Richards, *A New Face,* 50.

6. Howard A. Snyder, *The Problem of Wineskins* (Downers Grove, Ill.: InterVarsity, 1975), 70.

7. Kirk C. Hadaway, Francis M. DuBose, and Stuart A. Wright, *Home Cell Groups and House Churches* (Nashville: Broadman Press, 1987), 77.

8. Jim Petersen, *Church without Walls* (Colorado Springs: NavPress, 1992), 173–174.

9. Ibid., 214.

10. Jim Petersen, *Lifestyle Discipleship* (Colorado Springs: NavPress, 1993), 85.

Chapter 3: Making Disciples

1. Bob Russell, *God's Message for a Growing Church* (Cincinnati: Standard Publishing, 1990), 7–8.

2. Charles R. Swindoll, *Dropping Your Guard: The Value of Open Relationships*: 350–501; reprinted in *The Inspirational Writings of Charles R. Swindoll* (New York: Inspirational Press, 1988), 367.

3. Paul Yonggi Cho and Harold Hostetler, *Successful Home Cell Groups* (Plainfield, N.J.: Logos International, 1981), 67. Cho changed his first name to David in 1992 (C. Peter Wagner, "People & Events,"

"Yonggi Cho Changes His Name," *Charisma*, November 1992), 80.

4. *The Lookout* is a weekly magazine for Christian adults published by Standard Publishing, 8121 Hamilton Avenue, Cincinnati, Ohio 45231. (800) 543-1353.

5. C. Peter Wagner, *Your Church Can Grow*, rev. ed. (Ventura, Calif.: Regal Books, 1984), 86.

Chapter 4: The Growing Influence of Small Groups

1. Much of the material for this historical summary comes from Lyman Coleman's "Growing the Church through Small Groups" notebook from the seminar held March 10–13, 1987, at Fuller Theological Seminary, Pasadena, California, and from a personal interview with Coleman, February 26, 1993. Coleman has been involved in the small group movement and has led training seminars for more than thirty years.

2. This chapter is not exhaustive of all small group knowledge. It is assumed that the reader has a basic understanding of small group types, terminology, curriculum, promotion, child care, and other organizational matter. Many books give particulars about leading and organizing small groups. This chapter will not rehash the information in those books.

3. George Barna, "Small Groups Are Getting Smaller: Is the 'Church of Tomorrow' Falling Apart Today?" *Ministry Currents* (April/June 1993): 12.

4. George Barna, *The Barna Report 1992–93* (Ventura, Calif.: Regal Books, 1992), 281.

5. George Barna, *Absolute Confusion: How Our Moral and Spiritual Foundations Are Eroding in This Age of Change* (Ventura, Calif.: Regal Books, 1993), 288.

6. Robert Wuthnow, "How Small Groups Are Transforming Our Lives," *Christianity Today* (February 7, 1994): 21–24.

7. Julie A. Gorman, "Close Encounters: The Real Thing," *Christian Education Journal* 13, no. 3 (spring 1993): 10.

8. Roberta Hestenes, "Small Groups and the Revitalization of the Church," *Theology News and Notes* (October 1977): 29.

9. Cho and Hostetler, *Successful Home Cell Groups*, 50.

10. Lewis A. Coser, *Masters of Sociological Thought*, 2d ed. (San Diego: Harcourt Brace Jovanovich, 1977), 307. Coser quotes from Charles Horton Cooley, *Social Organization* (New York: Schocken, 1962), 23.

11. Ibid., 308.

12. Ibid., 309. Quote from Cooley, 30.

13. Lyman Coleman, "Growing the Church through Small Groups" conference, 26 February 1993.

14. Hestenes, "Small Groups and the Revitalization," 33.

15. Carl George, *Prepare Your Church for the Future* (Grand Rapids: Revell, 1991), 99.

16. Haydn Shaw, "Small Groups: The Shape of Things to Come," *Visionary* 6, no. 2 (1991): 4.

17. J. Gregory Lawson, "The Utilization of Home Cell Groups," *Christian Education Journal* 13, no. 3 (spring 1993): 72.

18. Ron Johnson, telephone interview, 14 January 1991.

19. George, *Prepare Your Church for the Future*, 113.

20. Robert Wuthnow, *Sharing the Journey: Support Groups and America's Quest for Community* (New York: The Free Press, 1994), 27.

Chapter 5: Is There a Future for the Sunday School?

1. Jerry M. Stubblefield, *A Church Ministering to Adults* (Nashville: Broadman Press, 1986), 165–66.

2. James DeForest Murch, *Christian Education in the Local Church*, rev. ed. (Cincinnati: Standard Publishing, 1958), 66.

3. Warren Bird, "The Great Small-Group Takeover," *Christianity Today* (February 7, 1994): 27.

4. Arn, McGavran, and Arn, *Growth*, 20.

5. Ibid., 29.

6. Ibid., 25–26.

7. Steve G. Fortosis, "A Review of the Reasons for Adult Education Participation and Implications for the Local Church," *Christian Education Journal* 12, no. 2 (winter 1992): 99.

8. Lyle E. Schaller, *Hey, That's Our Church!* (1975; reprint, Nashville: Abingdon Press, 1978), 143.

9. Arn, McGavran, and Arn, *Growth*, 29, 33.

10. Ibid., 40.

11. Howard A. Snyder, *Liberating the Church: The Ecology of Church and Kingdom* (Downers Grove, Ill.: InterVarsity, 1983), 161.

12. Elmer Towns, "The Nine Futures of Sunday School," *The Church Growth Newsletter* 4, no. 1:2.

13. Wagner, *Your Church Can Grow*, 120.

14. Hadaway, DuBose, and Wright, *Home Cell Groups and House Churches*, 61.

15. George, *Prepare Your Church for the Future*, 47.

16. Walden Howard, compiler, *Groups That Work: The Key to Renewal . . . for Churches, Communities, and Individuals!* (1967; reprint, Grand Rapids: Zondervan, 1972), 56.

17. George, *Prepare Your Church for the Future*, 77.

18. Towns, "The Nine Futures of Sunday School," 2.

19. George Barna, *What Americans Believe: An Annual Survey of Values and Religious Views in the United States* (Ventura, Calif.: Regal Books, 1991), 280–81.

20. Paul Benjamin, *The Growing Congregation* (1972; reprint, Cincinnati: Standard Publishing, 1975), 31–33.

21. Paul Benjamin, *The Equipping Ministry* (Cincinnati: Standard Publishing, 1978), 49.

22. Ontology is the science or study of the nature of being or existence. Functionalism has to do with the idea that things should serve a practical use. Contemporary American society has shifted from ontology to functionalism. That is, most people care more about what a person can *do* than who a person *is*.

23. Towns, "The Nine Futures of Sunday School," 3.

24. Elmer L. Towns, "How to Reach the Baby Boomer," (notebook for seminar presented in Covington, Kentucky, 1990), 42.

25. Towns, "The Nine Futures of Sunday School," 2–3.

26. Research by Cole and Glass, Knowles, and Wlodowski is presented in "A Review of Reasons for Adult Education Participation and Implications for the Local Church," by Steve Fortosis, 95. He also refers to research by Johnson and Rivera that shows that adults seek practical, skill-oriented teaching. Also, he cites research by Klinger, Cross, and Rossing and Young, who each identify that adults will usually participate in learning activities only if they find them meaningful, emotionally significant, and life-related to them.

Chapter 6: Sunday School and Small Groups Side by Side

1. Barna Research Group, "The Small Group Letter," *Discipleship Journal* (1 November 1987): 43.

2. John N. Vaughan, "North America's Fastest Growing Churches," *Church Growth Today* 6, no. 6 (1992): 2–3.

3. The figure for the percentage of growing churches with traditional adult Sunday school programs agrees with other research on Sunday schools. The

Yearbook of American and Canadian Churches reports that 140,000 of 200,000 Protestant congregations (70 percent) operate Sunday school programs.

4. Elmer L. Towns, "Evangelism in the Nineties," *Church Growth Newsletter* 2, no. 1: 2.

5. Stubblefield, *A Church Ministering to Adults*, 167.

6. Ibid.

7. Robert E. Coleman, *Master Plan of Evangelism* (1963; reprint, Grand Rapids: Revell, 1987), 112.

8. Towns, "The Nine Futures of Sunday School," 3.

9. Cho and Hostetler, *Successful Home Cell Groups*, 58.

10. Ibid., 62–63.

11. Jeffrey Arnold, *The Big Book on Small Groups* (Downers Grove, Ill.: InterVarsity, 1992), 23.

12. Ibid., 32.

13. Paul Meier et al., *Filling the Holes in Our Souls* (Chicago: Moody, 1992), 44.

14. George, *Prepare Your Church for the Future*, 60.

15. Coser, *Masters of Sociological Thought*, 188.

16. Martha M. Leypoldt, *Learning Is Change* (Valley Forge, Penn.: Judson Press, 1971), 67.

17. Lawrence O. Richards, *A Theology of Christian Education* (Grand Rapids: Zondervan, 1975), 318.

18. Arnold, *The Big Book on Small Groups*, 120–21.

Chapter 7: Either-Or or Both-And?

1. George, *Prepare Your Church for the Future*, 67.

2. Ibid., 118.

3. Wagner, *Your Church Can Grow*, 111–25.

4. Ibid., 123.

5. John Vaughan, telephone interview, 27 February 1992.

6. "The Small Group Letter," *Discipleship Journal* 65 (1991): 52.

Chapter 8: Traditional Churches in Transition

1. Simon J. Dahlman, "Alive and Well," *The Lookout* (July 24, 1994): 14.

2. Elmer L. Towns, *Ten Sunday Schools That Dared to Change: How Churches across America Are Changing Paradigms to Reach a New Generation* (Ventura, Calif.: Regal Books, 1993).

3. Schaller, *The Seven-Day-a-Week Church*.

4. Thom and Joani Schultz, *Why Nobody Learns Much of Anything at Church: And How to Fix It* (Loveland, Colo.: Group, 1993), 141.

5. Ibid., 218.

6. Barna, *User Friendly*, 16.

7. Hadaway, DuBose, and Wright, *Home Cell Groups and House Churches*, 129–40.

8. Towns, "How to Reach the Baby Boomer," 45.

9. Lowell Goetze, "Programs Do Not Make Disciples," *NewService*, Churches Alive (summer 1992): 4.

Chapter 10: How Each Group Works with the Whole Body

1. George Barna, *The Frog in the Kettle: What Christians Need to Know about Life in the Year 2000* (Ventura, Calif.: Regal Books, 1990), 95.

2. Lyman Coleman, *Small Group Training Manual* (Littleton, Colo.: Serendipity House, 1991), 25.

3. Cho and Hostetler, *Successful Home Cell Groups*, 108–9.

4. Lyle E. Schaller, *Looking in the Mirror: Self-Appraisal in the Local Church* (Nashville: Abingdon Press, 1984), 145–46.

Chapter 11: Making the Changes

1. Barna Research Group, "The New Generation of Leaders—The Maturing of Baby Boomers," *Christian Marketing Perspective* 3, no. 2 (spring 1987): 2.

2. Barna, *The Frog in the Kettle*, 43.

3. Richards, *A New Face*, 180.

4. George, *Prepare Your Church for the Future*, 113.

5. Roberta Hestenes, *Turning Committees into Communities* (Colorado Springs: NavPress, 1991), 6.

6. Schaller, *Looking in the Mirror*, 151.

7. Joe S. Ellis, *The Church on Target: Achieving Your Congregation's Highest Potential* (Cincinnati: Standard Publishing, 1986), 59.

Bibliography

Anderson, Leith. *Dying for Change*. Minneapolis: Bethany, 1990.

Arn, Charles, and Win Arn. *The Master Plan for Making Disciples*. Pasadena, Calif.: Church Growth Press, 1982.

Arnold, Jeffrey. *The Big Book on Small Groups*. Downers Grove, Ill.: InterVarsity, 1992.

Barker, Steve, et al. *Good Things Come in Small Groups: The Dynamics of Good Group Life*. Downers Grove, Ill.: InterVarsity, 1985.

———. *Small Group Leaders' Handbook*. Downers Grove, Ill.: InterVarsity, 1982.

Barna, George. *The Frog in the Kettle: What Christians Need to Know about Life in the Year 2000*. Ventura, Calif.: Regal Books, 1990.

———. *Turnaround Churches: How to Overcome Barriers to Growth and Bring New Life to an Established Church*. Ventura, Calif.: Regal Books, 1993.

———. *User Friendly Churches: What Christians Need to Know about the Churches People Love to Go To*. Ventura, Calif.: Regal Books, 1991.

Cho, Paul Yonggi, and Harold Hostetler. *Successful Home Cell Groups*. Plainfield, N.J.: Logos International, 1981.

Coleman, Lyman, et al., eds. *The NIV Serendipity Bible for Study Groups*. 2d ed. Grand Rapids: Zondervan, 1989.

Coleman, Robert E. *The Master Plan of Discipleship*. Grand Rapids: Revell, 1987.

———. *The Master Plan of Evangelism*. 1963. Reprint. Grand Rapids: Revell, 1987.

Dudley, Carl S. *Making the Small Church Effective*. 1978. Reprint. Nashville: Abingdon Press, 1986.

Ellas, John W. *Church Growth through Groups: Strategies for Varying Levels of Christian Community*. Searcy, Ark.: Resource Publications, 1990.

Ellis, Joe S. *The Church on Target: Achieving Your Congregation's Highest Potential*. Cincinnati: Standard Publishing, 1986.

Galloway, Dale E. *20/20 Vision: How to Create a Successful Church*. Portland, Ore.: Scott Publishing Company, 1986.

Galvin, James C., sen. ed. *The Small Group Study Bible*. Wheaton: Tyndale, 1995.

George, Carl F. *Prepare Your Church for the Future*. Grand Rapids: Revell, 1991.

Gorman, Julie A., gen. ed. *A Training Manual for Small Group Leaders*. Wheaton: Victor, 1991.

Hadaway, C. Kirk, Francis M. DuBose, and Stuart A. Wright. *Home Cell Groups and House Churches*. Nashville: Broadman Press, 1987.

Hamlin, Judy. *The Small Group Leader's Training Course*. Colorado Springs: NavPress, 1990.

Hartman, Warren J. *Five Audiences*. Ed. Lyle E. Schaller. Creative Leadership Series. Nashville: Abingdon Press, 1987.

Hestenes, Roberta. *Building Christian Community through Small Groups*. Pasadena, Calif.: Fuller Theological Seminary, n.d. Cassettes and Course Syllabus.

———. *Turning Committees into Communities*. Colorado Springs: NavPress, 1991.

———. *Using the Bible in Groups*. Philadelphia: The Westminster Press, 1983.

Hipp, Jeanne. *How to Start and Grow Small Groups in Your Church*. Monrovia, Calif.: Church Growth, Inc., 1989.

Hull, Bill. *The Disciple Making Church*. Grand Rapids: Revell, 1990.

McBride, Neal. *How to Build a Small Groups Ministry*. Colorado Springs: NavPress, 1995.

———. *How to Lead Small Groups*. Colorado Springs: NavPress, 1990.

McGavran, Donald A. *Understanding Church Growth*. Rev. ed. Grand Rapids: Eerdmans, 1980.

McGavran, Donald, and Win Arn. *How to Grow Your Church: Conversations about Church Growth*. Ventura, Calif.: Regal Books, 1973.

Meier, Paul, et al. *Filling the Holes in Our Souls*. Chicago: Moody, 1992.

Navigators, eds. *How to Lead Small Group Bible Studies*. Colorado Springs: NavPress, 1982.

Petersen, Jim. *Church without Walls*. Colorado Springs: NavPress, 1992.

———. *Lifestyle Discipleship*. Colorado Springs: NavPress, 1993.

———. *Living Proof*. Colorado Springs: NavPress, 1989.

Proctor, Frank. *Growing the Church through an Effective Church School*. St. Louis: CBP Press, 1990.

Richards, Lawrence O. *Creative Bible Teaching*. Chicago: Moody, 1970.

———. *A New Face for the Church*. Grand Rapids: Zondervan, 1970.

Schaller, Lyle E., ed. *Assimilating New Members*. Nashville: Abingdon Press, 1978.

———. *Growing Pains*. 1983. Reprint. Nashville: Abingdon Press, 1984.

———. *Hey, That's Our Church!* 1975. Reprint. Nashville: Abingdon Press, 1978.

———. *Looking in the Mirror: Self-Appraisal in the Local Church.* Nashville: Abingdon Press, 1984.

———. *The Seven-Day-a-Week Church.* Nashville: Abingdon Press, 1992.

Schultz, Thom, and Joani Schultz. *Why Nobody Learns Much of Anything at Church: And How to Fix It.* Loveland, Colo.: Group, 1993.

Seemuth, David P. *How Dynamic Is Your Small Group?* Wheaton: Victor, 1991.

Sikora, Pat. *Small Group Bible Studies: How to Lead Them.* Cincinnati: Standard Publishing, 1991.

Snyder, Howard A. *Liberating the Church: The Ecology of Church and Kingdom.* Downers Grove, Ill.: InterVarsity, 1983.

———. *The Problem of Wineskins: Church Structure in a Technological Age.* Downers Grove, Ill.: InterVarsity, 1975.

Towns, Elmer L. *An Inside Look at 10 of Today's Most Innovative Churches.* Ventura, Calif.: Regal Books, 1990.

Towns, Elmer, John N. Vaughan, and David J. Seifert. *The Complete Book of Church Growth.* Wheaton: Tyndale, 1981.

Vaughan, John N. *The Large Church: A Twentieth-Century Expression of the First-Century Church.* Grand Rapids: Baker, 1985.

Wagner, C. Peter. *Leading Your Church to Growth.* Ventura, Calif.: Regal Books, 1984.

———. *Your Church Can Grow.* 1976. Rev. ed. Ventura, Calif.: Regal Books, 1984.

Williams, Dan. *Seven Myths about Small Groups: How to Keep from Falling into Common Traps.* Downers Grove, Ill.: InterVarsity, 1991.

Wuthnow, Robert. *Sharing the Journey: Support Groups and America's New Quest for Community.* New York: The Free Press, 1994.

Index

Michael C. Mack operates The Small Group Network, Inc., an organization that provides training and support for small group leaders. (The Small Group Network is on the World Wide Web at http://smallgroups.com.) Michael has been involved in small group and adult Sunday school leadership, and he writes for several national magazines. He lives in Cincinnati, Ohio, with his wife, Heidi, and their three children.